MOVING THROUGH LIFE

UNIVERSITY PRESS OF FLORIDA

Florida A&M University, Tallahassee
Florida Atlantic University, Boca Raton
Florida Gulf Coast University, Ft. Myers
Florida International University, Miami
Florida State University, Tallahassee
New College of Florida, Sarasota
University of Central Florida, Orlando
University of Florida, Gainesville
University of North Florida, Jacksonville
University of South Florida, Tampa
University of West Florida, Pensacola

Moving through Life

Essential Lessons of Dance

Naomi Goldberg Haas

with Mikhaela Mahony

UNIVERSITY PRESS OF FLORIDA

Gainesville/Tallahassee/Tampa/Boca Raton
Pensacola/Orlando/Miami/Jacksonville/Ft. Myers/Sarasota

30 29 28 27 26 25   6 5 4 3 2 1

Library of Congress Cataloging-in-Publication Data
Names: Goldberg Haas, Naomi, author. | Mahony, Mikhaela, contributor.
Title: Moving through life : essential lessons of dance / Naomi Goldberg
Haas with Mikhaela Mahony.
Description: 1. | Gainesville : University Press of Florida, 2025. |
Includes bibliographical references.
Identifiers: LCCN 2024038403 (print) | LCCN 2024038404 (ebook) | ISBN
9780813080956 (paperback) | ISBN 9780813073705 (ebook)
Subjects: LCSH: Goldberg Haas, Naomi. | Modern dance—United
States—Biography. | Dancers—United States—Biography. |
Choreographers—United States—Biography. | BISAC: PERFORMING ARTS /
Dance / General | SELF-HELP / Aging
Classification: LCC GV1785.G6184 A3 2025 (print) | LCC GV1785.G6184
(ebook) | DDC 792.802/8092 [B]—dc23/eng/20240917
LC record available at https://lccn.loc.gov/2024038403
LC ebook record available at https://lccn.loc.gov/2024038404

The University Press of Florida is the scholarly publishing agency for the State University System
of Florida, comprising Florida A&M University, Florida Atlantic University, Florida Gulf Coast
University, Florida International University, Florida State University, New College of Florida, University of Central Florida, University of Florida, University of North Florida, University of South
Florida, and University of West Florida.

University Press of Florida
2046 NE Waldo Road
Suite 2100
Gainesville, FL 32609
http://upress.ufl.edu

For Brian Kulick, my husband, whose unflagging faith and support made this book possible through the differences and similarities we share as people, artists, lovers, and friends.

CONTENTS

Prelude

Life is movement. Effortlessly, we move through time from the moment we are born. Our days move from childhood to young adulthood, to the richness of adult life, to the close of our days as elders of society. Embracing life as a whole is embracing a sense of movement, and as I have traveled through the flow of time, I have embraced this movement quite literally. I am a dancer. I have practiced endlessly reaching, walking, sitting, standing, moving with grace. To me, the essential lessons of life are the essential lessons of dance.

Dance is an open conversation with the body and the way it moves through both space and time. Dance does not lie—one can only move within the realities of one's own particular body. It is common for us, as we age, to view these realities as limitations. In fact, it is common for us to view a lot of our circumstances as we age through such a narrow lens. We look at our lives as though they were an ever-shrinking circle. There is this fear, maybe we are aware of it, maybe it lies beneath the surface. There is a fear that we are in a state of loss. As we get older, our eyesight gets worse. Our limbs become harder to move as our muscles naturally weaken and at the same time become less fluid. It is as though someone fiddled with the volume in our ears without our permission. Our bodies change. We lose mobility. Time takes things from us: the acuity of our senses, our facility with words and memories, our dear friends and loved ones. Dance, however, is not loss, but gain. Dance is a gift back to the body. The study and practice of dance is an opportunity for renewal and regrowth. It is an opportunity to reshape, to move differently, but no less fully. The work that I do celebrates the imagination, and the impulse to move in alternate ways. "Alternate" is an essential word in my work. Alternate represents a choice to open up your thinking, not to think and move in terms of what you cannot do, but to think in terms of what you can, where you are capable of moving forward. This is your body right now, and it is up to you to move forward in whatever way makes sense to you. Move whatever you can move. All movement is good. The body feels slightly different every day, but you strengthen your awareness of your own body with each dance experience. It is this connection to your body—in the precise moment of movement—that is unique to dance. Knowing you will change and change again is an empowering element of thinking like a dancer. And thinking in this way, I believe, leads to greater happiness, fulfillment, and gratitude throughout the areas of one's life. I have good reason to put faith in this idea. As you read these pages, you will chart the course of my life. You will hear about my young life as an emerging dancer. You will also hear about my life now, as a woman battling a degenerative disease—a disease that makes movement increasingly difficult for me. I believe that both of these chapters of my life contain equally vital lessons about dance. Because of my disease, I have lived the challenges that older people face as their bodies change. I am not speaking in theory; I am speaking the truth of my life. In so doing, I know that I can speak uniquely to dance's transformative power: no matter your age, no matter your ability.

I felt called upon to write this book, to share the value of living in the world as a dancer, and how that can be meaningful for all people. I know the truth of this intimately. The ideology and pedagogy in this book are very closely linked to the curriculum I developed with my New York City–based company. When we founded the company in 2005, we chose the name Dances for a Variable Population (DVP) in order to honor the dancers in all of us, both on stage and in the audience. We wanted dance to be an active word, not owned by any one group, but to be noted as all-inclusive. The methodology developed through years of classes with DVP has become Movement Speaks®. Its goals are to share movements drawn from a variety of dance forms (classical, modern, folk, and contemporary), fitness, and most importantly ways to activate personal expression. We believe that such an exploration engenders greater physical and mental health while promoting social connection and improved quality of life for all.

This book will introduce the core tenets of physical awareness, developing a mind-body connection, and building strength, mobility, balance, and confidence in personal choice. Alternating between teacher-led movement and self-directed movement, the core program of the book introduces how the exercises originated and were developed, and the important rationales they offer. The Essential Lessons of Dance shares the

Movement Speaks method in an expanded toolbook of how the joyous discovery of dance is within you and comes from all the years of your life.

When I began writing this book with Mikhaela Mahony, our goal was simple: to relay the exercises that make up the class to a larger population. But as I continued working and writing, it became clear to me that these exercises are more than a guide for accomplishing specific movements: they are an amalgamation of all the lessons that my life in dance has rendered, be they physical or philosophical. These are practices I have learned while studying, making, and thinking about myself as a dancer. As a result, this book is many things: part practical manual of movement; part manifesto on the broader implications of learned principles such as balance, flexibility, and creativity; and part personal autobiography.

But before we begin, it might be helpful to have a very brief overview of where I am coming from. I trained at the New York City School of American Ballet from the age eight to eighteen, and while this was my formative foundation and remains one of my first reference points in relation to dance, it was just the beginning of a long and wonderful journey toward discovering the many ways our bodies can move through space. I am the beneficiary of an amazing moment in the history of dance, a veritable explosion of dance forms that I could not resist experiencing, studying, performing, and incorporating into my own work. This includes borrowings from the high priests and priestesses of modern dance, titans like Martha Graham and her contractions, Merce Cunningham and his chance operations, and José Limón and his trademark fall and recovery technique. Equally influential was the impact of contemporary postmodern dance, beginning with the invigorating nonchalance of the Judson Church movement, which included Steve Paxton, David Gordon, and Yvonne Rainer. This was followed by kindred dance spirits like Trisha Brown, Meredith Monk, Elizabeth Keen, and Phyllis Lamhut; and, a generation later, Mark Morris with his musicality. In the midst of all this was the inspiration from the German invasion, which first landed at Brooklyn Academy of Music with Pina Bausch, and all those different body types united in their deadpan whimsy and virtuosity; followed by the wild derring-do of Sasha Waltz; the pristine wizardly of Anna De Keersmaeker; and the final sucker-punch of William Forsyth and the Frankfurt Ballet, which knocked me out when I first saw their work. In each of these movement systems I have found an invaluable concept that became a tool to add to my ever-expanding dance-toolbox, enabling me to build all manner of dances. My ultimate idea of dance, to switch metaphors, exists under a huge imaginary tent where everyone is invited to share the way they move and to learn from one another in the process.

Now, a little more about this book: you have a choice in using it the way it is laid out, in order of events, or simply pick out the various exercises as they are described. The initial exercises that correspond to Part One (Beginning Steps) can be found in the back of the book. These exercises begin with a fundamental understanding of how breath works. From there we move on to exercises in grounding yourself in your body, building strength, increasing flexibility, finding balance, and experiencing the joys of proprioception (a big word for simply knowing where your body is in space). You do not have to read any of the preceding chapters to understand or execute any given exercise, as they are self-contained and self-explanatory; but we encourage you, if you have the time, to read the chapters that precede each set of exercises. These chapters will give you a larger experiential and philosophical context for why such exercises can be helpful and why they are sequenced the way they are. You will also find instructions corresponding to Parts Two (Intermezzo), Three (All Together Now), and Four (The *Grande Finale*) for responding to others, working in groups, developing choreographic tools, implementing techniques of improvisations, and learning about various structures for making your own dances. This is another, more creative, set of exercises; equally beneficial to one's body, but also developing the reader's collaborative skills, imagination, and inspiring the inner choreographer that hides inside each of us. Put all four parts of the book together with the corresponding exercises and the reader can gain a 360-degree understanding of our approach to movement. While not an exact carbon copy, the structure of the book mirrors the structure of a Movement Speaks course, and many Movement Speaks students are included among its pages. The names of these and other individuals have been changed unless they granted permission for their inclusion. When practicing these movements, adjust for what speaks to you personally for your own practice as a dancer, dance teacher, caregiver, learner, human being. The practice of living as a dancer can be a part of everyone's life—you can embrace moving with the awareness of possibility and connection, whether you take Movement Speaks classes by yourself or with a caregiver, among new friends, or with your family.

As you embark on this journey, before you turn the page, it is important that you acknowledge to yourself, as a new older dancer, or a seasoned dancer later in life, or a teacher of movement: you have a choice. When taking a dance class at a young age, many are told to be there by your parents. As an adult, you choose to be here for yourself.

This book elucidates the reasons why to be here, why to choose to move, and how to choose yourself. Choosing movement instills a sense of joy, partnership, grace, and an appreciation for your own body. Choosing movement means experiencing better balance, developing your strength, gaining flexibility and mobility, boosting your confidence, and deepening your own creative mastery. It is essential that older adults feel stronger and happier. It is vital that they feel their bodies are changing in increasingly positive ways, and their minds are sharpening. This book will aid you in developing a sense of ownership and reasons to continue practicing. Move from a place of curiosity and pleasure. Let yourself be taken by surprise. Whether you discover newfound strength, balance, or confidence, be open to what can grow from this work, the work of dancing.

1

BEGINNING STEPS

Naomi dancing at Pacific Northwest Ballet. Photo © Archie K. Horspool, 1981, for
Pacific Northwest Ballet.

In the Beginning

The scene was almost like an optical illusion, a magic eye puzzle. Before my eyes was a dizzying kaleidoscope: a sea of black and pink and white. A mass of young ballerinas. The only way to cut through the chaos of small bodies and tulle was the numbers pinned on the fronts of each girl's leotard. I stood among them with a number pinned on me, too. I looked down. Number 242. I was momentarily reassured—OK, I'm me. My edges are secure, I won't get swallowed up by the colors and sounds and people. I am here, I am 242. I'm no one else, and no one else is me. To calm myself down before the audition, I invented a game. To keep my brain occupied, organized, and connected to the real world, I would pick out people from the roiling, dancing, stretching crowd and sort them into recognizable categories. I would get my mind in order. It was essentially a version of "I Spy," but exclusively for eight-year-old ballet dancers who found themselves auditioning for the School of American Ballet. She's blonde, she has dark hair, she's tall, she has a birthmark, she's holding her mother's hand, her mother is adjusting her ballet slipper. I had found one more element that defined me, separated me from the group. Each girl had her mother with her . . . but I was alone. Where was she? I began to grow nervous again. I wanted the audition to start as soon as possible, so I could begin dancing and stopped thinking. Yes, that felt like the best plan.

And then all of a sudden, we were swept into the room. We must have looked like a tidal wave of tiny ballerinas—black, pink, white, pink, pink, black, white. We lined up on the barre. My hand rested lightly on the wood. I took a deep breath. This was it, the moment. I had the sense that something massive and important was happening, that I was on the threshold of achieving my lifelong dream. I was about to enter the third grade, only eight years old. It is a lot of pressure for someone so young to put on themselves. But in that moment, poised at the barre, I felt like my whole life lay in the balance.

We began to move. Madame Dudin, a petite woman who spoke English with a French accent, led us in a series of exercises. She tested our flexibility, the rotation of our hips and legs, the elegance of our feet and arches.

"You. Number 242. Point your toes."

I did.

"Hmmm. Not a very high instep. Number 243?"

I lowered my head to look down at my foot. A low arch. I had never looked at my body before with anything except pride, at best, or at worst, a neutral inattention. It had not occurred to me to notice flaws. In my mind, it had always just been my body, my way of dancing and moving. But now I was Number 242, and Number 242 had bad arches, so I judged this Number 242 person and her subpar feet. For perhaps the first time, I was disappointed in my body.

No sooner had Madame Dudin passed me over than Madame Tumkovsky arrived to extend my leg and determine my flexibility.

"Higher! Higher!"

These are the words forever etched into my brain when I summon an image of Madame Tumkovsky. Her English was limited, but she certainly knew which words were the most important.

"Higher! Leg higher!"

I did not need more language than that to understand what she meant. I continued to extend my leg, to try and be the body that would please these teachers. I was not focused on my arches anymore; now I was focused on my legs and hips. There was no time to dwell on my newfound self-judgment, and it stealthily slipped away to find some quiet place to rest inside my psyche until it was called upon again.

Madame Stuart released us from the barre and led us in waltzes on a diagonal line across the floor. In this movement, I was home. For the first time that day, I felt free. The music lifted me up and I could match my movements with the sounds, and I felt like I was in the right place at the right time. It all synched. I looked over at Madame Stuart and immediately fell in love with her. Finally, a Madame I could understand.

And just as quickly as it had all begun, it was over. The tide of aspiring dancers ebbed. With what felt like a single exhale, we all spilled out of Lincoln Center with our mothers and evaporated into the city. I wondered how many girls would be admitted into the school. I wondered if I would be one of them.

To my great delight, I was.

"Classes are how often?"

I stood nervously behind the door as my mother spoke on the phone. I just happened to be passing by as she was talking to Madame Natalie Gleboff, the school administrator for the School of American Ballet, and figured it wouldn't hurt just to linger by the door.

"Three times per week?"

And so far, I was not loving what I was hearing. Judging by my mother's voice, the conversation did not sound like it was coming out in my favor.

"I need to drive into the city three times a week? You've got to be kidding me. She's eight!"

The School of American Ballet was not an ordinary dance school, and therefore did not put forward ordinary demands on students' time. Regardless of the age of the dancers, the training was rigorous and disciplined; and, as such, much more frequent than the kind of after-school dance program you might imagine for an eight-year-old learning ballet. As I continued to listen to my mother on the phone, it started to become clear that the time commitment suggested that this school for dance might take away from my studies at my actual school—and if that was the case, I knew I was done for. My mother put incredible value in education; she was even studying to become a teacher of teachers. I thought then that if enrolling in School of American Ballet meant a choice between my academics and my dancing, I was cooked.

Thankfully for me, that was not the only conversation my mother was having about my balletic ambitions. My mother was currently pursuing an Ed.D. at Columbia University's Teacher's College under the advisement of Maxine Greene, a famed educator and a fan of the ballet. Maxine told my mother that acceptance to the School of American Ballet was an enormous honor, and that we should be very proud. Her approval, combined with my deep desire for focused training, convinced my parents. That was that. In September, I began my training at the School of American Ballet.

Only now do I see the irony in Maxine Greene's role in my dance education fate. Maxine Greene's education philosophy was rooted in creative learning. She was a constant innovator and barrier-breaker, defying expectations as a female leader in higher education and reinventing long-accepted but rarely questioned educational models. Her educational philosophy was centered around student involvement and inquisitiveness—she thought the best way to teach was to encourage question-asking and student-led projects. It seems strange to me now that

The Bryant School's Balanchine, Naomi Goldberg, eleven, floats through a ballet jump in a performance for her Teaneck, N.J., friends on May 29, 1972. Naomi organized, directed, and choreographed the day's ballet recital. From the *Bergen County Record*. © Gordon Corbett—USA TODAY NETWORK.

this renowned advocate for student freedom was also an advocate for the School of American Ballet, which in my experience did not support student freedom. A different kind of vision is required to be clear in the present, and an entirely new sense to be clear in the present in the body. But it would take me years, and a voyage to France, to discover exactly what that sense was.

Sensing the Mind-Body Connection

"An undisciplined colt." Those were the words of the great ballerina Rosella Hightower, director of the Centre de Danse International Rosella Hightower (as it was then called) in Cannes, as spoken to me, a twelve-year-old dancer in her summer program. An undisciplined colt. "Colt" seemed promising; I loved to dance more than anything and poured all my young energy into it. "Undisciplined . . ." perhaps not so promising. Rosella's words pinpointed a kind of lack of organization in my body—energy, but without awareness. The critique stung, but she was right. Physically disorganized was exactly how I felt at the time. I had come to study that summer not simply to perfect my technique or train my body—I had come hoping for a remedy.

Months before, I had been diagnosed with scoliosis, just as my older sister Lisa had. ("Genetics," my mother said.) The effects of the disease were increasing radically, and X-rays showed that I was headed toward wearing a back brace from neck to pelvis. I was terrified. I had been dancing at the School of American Ballet at Lincoln Center for nearly four years, dancing more days and more hours both because I loved it and also because I desperately wanted to achieve the perfect Balanchine body and style. Scoliosis would ruin all of that. My mother took me to France in an effort to alleviate my scoliosis. She hoped to protect my future in the world of ballet at best, and at worst, to give me the opportunity to dance one last time.

We traveled across the ocean and through France to arrive in a cold dormitory in Cannes, full of dancers who appeared to be around my age yet seemed much more worldly-wise. The students ranged from the children of the rich and famous, like the Estée Lauder girls, to the talented young ballerinas of L'Opera. I remember it all so clearly: the barre in a beautiful, well-used studio, the chandelier hanging in the hall. I remember barely being able to decipher the French instructions in my classes—my mother had assumed that since ballet terminology was all in French, I would be able to understand, but unfortunately this was not entirely the case. As such, it did not end up being the most social summer of my life. The language barrier was not my only problem, however. I was missing more than fluency in conversational French. I was missing fluency in my body.

Over the course of that month in July, however, something shifted. It was almost like learning a language, when you are not necessarily conscious of how much you are learning and then all of a sudden you sense a different understanding. My understanding of my body began to subtly change. I began to discover the idea of center. I started to diagnose my movements, began to feel what it was to extend my limbs from my center, to align myself with that center point. I began to feel when I was connected or disconnected from my center. All dancing should come from this aligned, connected place.

I left Cannes after the completion of the program at the end of the month. Upon my return, I revisited my doctors. The new X-rays showed that the way I used my back muscles to improve my alignment in dance had straightened my spine. I did not need to wear a back brace when I returned to the United States. My sister, however, went through years of therapeutic exercises in addition to wearing a back brace all through middle school and high school. Ballet taught me commitment to correct form and placement. It gave me a sense of power, a sense of knowing my body was magic. My body would always know what to do. This experience of body trust is what a dancer understands and is pivotal for life.

The following summer, my mother sent me to the Briansky Ballet in Saratoga Springs. Ironically, Saratoga Springs was the summer home of the New York City Ballet, and my relationship with my body deepened. That summer was a summer of sweat, elation, and excitement. It was in that funky, hot, humidly sweaty gym that I first experienced truly knowing what it means to sense turnout and rotation, to sense my leg absolutely straight, to sense the feeling of a line in the body. I could understand what a teacher meant when they said, "From the end of the foot to the tips of the fingers and beyond" when creating an arabesque. I could feel what it was to extend a leg forward and sense the rotation of the leg and the activation of the inner thigh and center. And I could feel the lift of the leg to the side while sensing rotation in order to achieve the lift, always aware of the muscles in the back of the leg. I could feel the spiraling of the muscles from inside to outside, know what being centered truly feels like, and understand, or accurately imagine, what being centered truly looks like.

During my summer in Saratoga Springs, I learned how to work as a dancer, both in terms of the discipline dance requires and the particular perspective dance demands. I had to learn a new way of seeing the shapes I was making on the outside while matching them with the physical work I was doing on the inside. A way to look inside and outside at the same time—I was my own X-ray now. I had learned to cultivate this inside-outside vision of myself as a dancer—namely, the ability to move and sense the picture I was creating with my body in space. Dancers perfect this imagination, this specific vantage point of an inside/outside point of view.

A dancer must have an image of how they look and match the position with how they feel, so that they know you are holding a straight spine, a connected line in an arabesque, a perfect passé. This is why mirrors can be so useful in dance studios—they are one's first understanding of how you look—but mirrors also take you out of yourself. They can place too much emphasis on the visual and divorce you from your feelings of you. The X-ray and the mirror both pose exciting framings of the somatic aspect of the dancer's perspective, the body as perceived within and outside.

I look back to those early summers often, in my own work as a dancer and in my work as a teacher. I see the influence in direct ways—these summers gave me the gift of knowing in my body: knowing how to stand, how to hold myself, how to dance, and how to live. I can also see the influence in less obvious but equally intuitive ways. I am always looking to replicate the feeling of that gym in Saratoga Springs, for example. I gravitate toward gymnasiums—school gyms and community organizations like Jewish Community Centers (JCCs) and YMCAs—where people really move, where regular people can walk in and dance without the baggage that comes with a formal studio, such as markers of tradition or class that can make people feel like they do not belong.

The inner knowledge of my body and how it manifested in an outward shape taught me how to live. It gave me a mind-body connection that I have relied on in dance and in life ever since. The mind-body connection should not be confused with René Descartes's mind-body dualism (sometimes referred to, rather ominously, as the mind-body *problem*). Descartes told us back in the seventeenth century that the mind and the body were, for all intents and purposes, independent of one another.[1] This theory had a major impact on both philosophy and science throughout Europe for the next several centuries. Many dancers, however, did not take the mind-body-separation very seriously and continued to assume that the mind and body were deeply connected, or at least on good terms with one another, resulting in what we now call the mind-body connection. Over the centuries, most dancers have quietly persevered in this basic belief, and it turns out, dancers were right all along. Thanks to the advances of modern neurobiology, we now know the mind-body separation that Descartes outlined is rather misguided; these two aspects of ourselves turn out to be irrevocably intertwined. Let us take a simple example: if you are in a good mood and catch your reflection in the mirror, chances are you will see that you are smiling. There is no great revelation in this, but neurobiologists have found that if you find yourself in a rather blue mood and just force yourself to smile, even though you may not feel like smiling, this simple action tends to help put you in a better frame of mind. Why do you have to see the smile? Smiling stimulates a serotonin/dopamine response to the brain. Because your mind is accustomed to associating this habitual movement with happiness, it sends streams of this deep-seated sensation back to the brain. Upon receiving this stimulus, the brain cannot help but inadvertently start feeling happy again. This, mind you, is just from a simple upward curvature of the lips! Imagine how the movement of other more significant parts of your body can affect something as seemingly intransigent as a foul mood. You could say that the mind and the body are engaged in an intricate dance, or—more scientifically—our mind/body performs a kind of infinite feedback loop which can be very hard to unplug.[2] This, of course, is reciprocal, and just as the body can liberate the mind, the mind—left to its own devious devices—can often dominate the body with all manner of ideas about what the body should or should not do.

The ancient sages who developed the practice of yoga had an implicit understanding of the powerful impact of the mind on the body. One of the key places they located the mind-body connection was in the simple act of breathing. My friend Susan Priver, of whom you will hear more throughout this book, has been teaching yoga for decades and begins every class with *pranayama* (breathwork). It is a simple practice to slow the chatter of the mind. She guides her students to listen to their breath so they can turn their attention inward. The breathwork is also a way of anchoring to the present, hence the body-mind connection. From there her class moves into *asanas* (postures), whether seated, standing, or on our knees in lunges, linking postures together in a way most bodies are capable of doing (with or without the help of props). This particular communication with body/mind is between the parasympathetic and sympathetic nervous systems via the vagus nerve, which comes from the brain. The communication with mind/body happens in the nervous system. The breath serves to stimulate the vagus nerve, supporting down regulation of the nervous system and helping us find presence. Susan believes that "the muscles and soft tissue hold so many of our held emotions and trauma. A yoga practice can help the student learn from their own body and perhaps let go of negative thinking, by working through held tension." And so, mind and body meet in our breath and in our muscles.

I believe the same dynamic is at work when we dance. Here dance, like yoga, helps us better appreciate the mind-body connection. In much of our day-to-day existence, we tend to alternate between the two, prioritizing one while often forgetting the other. Dance is one of those rare opportunities that allows us to recalibrate ourselves so that mind and body are on more equal footing, experiencing being at the very same instant from both vantage points. The goal of the mind-body connection is to become aware of this collaboration happening within us.

The connected feeling is not always there. As the years passed, I had to continue to seek it out, tease it out. I could get wrapped up in the distractions of how to get there and end up missing it completely. But the feeling of learning your body as a young person—encountering your body changing and growing and developing—is not so different from relearning your body as you age. I think of my student Arnold, an older man who is surprisingly comfortable getting around despite his obvious unsteadiness. Arnold is of average height, 5' 10" or so, and of slender build. He is a consistent student, often arriving every week for class at the library before his wife, Anna, who is also an exemplary student but with very different capabilities. Anna is as smooth in movement as Arnold is rocky. She was a former dancer in her college days, while he is new to the idea. Both are seeking better health through dance, though they approach it from polar opposite places. As I watch Arnold in class, I question what must have affected his movement so profoundly. Why is he so unsteady and yet seems a pillar of ungrounded strength? I wonder if Arnold has a sense of center that is compromised, if he knows his movements are unsteady. Does he sense losses of balance daily? Does he worry about falls? Does he understand center? Does he sense his body in balance?

Whether we are "undisciplined colts" because of youthful over-energy or because of loss of strength or control as we age, we all can find presence, beauty, and an awareness of our bodies through an increased mind-body connection. Watching Arnold's unsteadiness, I am concerned with his safety all the time, and yet he innately understands his limitations—how fast he can or cannot travel, how his pace informs his steadiness. His own sense of self provides great confidence in movement.

We each have our own individual relationships to our own minds and our own bodies, and building the connection between the two is essential to both expressive movement and safe movement as we age. This connection begins with the awareness of what we can do and what we cannot do. It is also deeply rooted in the breath—the breath is the source of our steadiness.

Even now, as you read this, you can remember that you are a breathing, working body in space. As you read these words, can you also feel the air moving in and out of your lungs? Notice this sensation. Notice, right now, how air is coming into your body. Sense it as it moves through the nose, down the throat, into the lungs, and then throughout your body. Bring this awareness to your shape as you sit, and read, and breathe. Can you feel the widening of the middle lobe of your lungs as you breathe? Experiment with the creation of space that breath brings to the inside of your body. Feel your breath expand your ribcage to the sides, widening under the armpits. Do you feel it? If you have your hands free, I invite you to place one or both of your hands to the sides of your ribcage and really feel the width of the filling of your lungs. Simply bring awareness there. Now sense the back of your body: breathe into that space. Can you feel the expansion into the back at the base of your ribcage? When was the last time you thought about this space in your back?

Tracking our breath is the first step to building a deep relationship with the body and becoming aware of the mind-body connection. This connection is vital as a dancer and also as a person moving through the world every day: it inspires awareness from a health perspective, but to me, it also inspires awe, gratitude, an appreciation for the gift of life. Your breath is a miracle! Your body changing and moving to accommodate that breath is also a miracle! It is such a gift to be alive—and paying attention to the daily, oft-ignored mechanics of the body is the first way to appreciate that gift.[3]

The exercises corresponding to this chapter stretch our somatic awareness—meaning the perception of our corporeal form—from our breath out toward our limbs and extremities. Taking this awareness and employing it to understand the sensations in the body makes the mind of a dancer. Take this opportunity to cultivate an understanding of how a movement looks on the outside and how it feels on the inside: this will build your mind-body connection. It begins with the breath, as we have done together, then slowly expands focus to opening different muscles, and then moves into how you feel when extending the limbs from the core or center, feeling the equal and opposite pulls of energy. It is this seed of awareness that you are developing that the greatest dancers constantly employ, and that grows into knowing what an arabesque feels like, a parallel brush of the leg versus a rotated dégagé, a passé motivated by the lift of the inner thigh, a connected waltz 3/4 rhythm, a swirling pirouette, a reach of an arm to the sky connected to the focus upward. It is a sense of how a movement looks, balanced by its awareness.

However, a strong mind-body connection does not necessarily mean you will do all of those dance techniques perfectly. You may be thinking, "Ah, yes, she means one must practice that sensation in order to eventually do it perfectly." There's an element of truth in that, yes! Practice is vital, and I believe in it deeply—but I am not referring to "practice makes perfect" now. A strong mind-body connection does not guarantee some abstract notion of perfection, rather a mind-body connection encourages an awareness of your own body and the way it moves best. This is in opposition to any adherence to traditional ballet's understanding of what might be "perfect."

When I was young, someone once quoted that classic Voltaire idea: "The perfect is the enemy of the good."[4] As a natural perfectionist, this line of thinking drove me crazy. Why be "good enough" when you could work to something excellent, be first in the class, stand up front, be praised by your teachers? After years at the School of American Ballet, in conjunction and juxtaposition with some of my other experiences, I learned why. Because an idea of perfection, of style over substance, can erode a mind-body connection. You can start to lose a sense of center, a clear somatic understanding of matching your inside with the outside, when the image of what you are trying to achieve is not grounded in an understanding of your body.

It is likely not a coincidence that I was having meaningful discoveries about my own mind-body connection through my experiences in France and Saratoga Springs. This was around the same time I started seeking teachers outside of the walls of the School of American Ballet. There was something dissonant occurring between the exciting developments I was making as a pre-teen dancer and the particular lessons I was learning at the School of American Ballet, and I wanted to find something more harmonizing. I sought teachers elsewhere while simultaneously continuing my studies. This concept was discouraged at the School of American Ballet. There, the teachers believed that the technique and tradition they were passing on to students brought strength and beauty. The attitude at the time was that any other methods of practice were simply wrong. Or at the least, they would surely muddy the training we were going for with alternate techniques. I, however, had my doubts. I was a curious student! Moreover, I knew other students who came from different parts of the country and the world who had studied with other teachers and seemed to be able to do everything the School of American Ballet asked of us stylistically, while also working from this place of center that I found so revolutionary and essential. I longed to find that feeling again, and so I chose to study with whoever could impart this information. I was going rogue. A rebel in pointe shoes.

To complement my new, aforementioned rebel tendencies, I chose to study with Finis Jhung; he too was an iconoclast. Finis had come up as a ballet dancer in the 1960s, dancing with the Joffrey Ballet and Harkness Ballet,[5] but in the late sixties he left the pursuit altogether to dedicate himself to Buddhism. He returned to dance as a teacher in the early 1970s, infusing his dance instruction with a Buddhist sensibility.[6] Finis was so different from my teachers at the School of American Ballet, and not only in his teaching practices and emphases. Where they were big personalities, total characters, Finis Jhung was calm and soft-spoken. In his classes, held in a second-floor studio, he would stand on a stage and use a microphone to communicate because he was so quiet. He calmly made corrections to our movements—not evaluating us based on style or physical beauty per se, but more focused on our physical awareness of center, our ability to feel our core connected to the feet and hands. In a recent interview, Finis said, "I try to instill in my students what we call in Buddhism 'a seeking spirit.' To learn the truth so that you can apply it and better yourself."[7]

With Finis, I nurtured my seeking spirit and learned to seek center in my body, my way.

I would bring this seeking philosophy back to our daily barre work in the School of American Ballet, secretly practicing this kind of awareness in my body. The problem was, if I were to truly embrace this grounded, strong, steady, connected form of movement, I would not be able to keep it a secret. I would have to change, visibly. And so I did. I started to abandon the parts of the School of American Ballet education that did not feel grounded in a strong center. Slowly at first, then more and more.

I knew when I performed a fifth position with my heels crossing the opposite foot, instead of the proper form with the toe of my front foot perfectly parallel and connected to the heel of my back foot and vice versa, that my days of dancing Balanchine were over. I could not do it anymore because I did not believe in it. My new fifth position was essentially the traditional third position, but I had too much awareness as a dancer now, as a person inside my body, to sacrifice physical health and strength for a "perfect look." I had felt the truth of center, and I would not close my heel to the opposite toe in fifth position as I was taught, compromising style over correct alignment. With this new positioning of my feet, I may have looked lazy, but in fact I was gathering more information. I could feel the floor underneath, I could push off from a steady position. One should feel your feet on the ground in order to feel flight. It is not as healthy to "skim the earth," as in the School of American Ballet style, where there is the possibility of sacrificing steadiness in order to find more speed. This approach is particularly dangerous for the older adult and promotes injury among young ballet dancers.

The French and Russian teachers at the School of American Ballet overlooked me after that. Suddenly, I was not placed front and center. It was painful, but I felt, in the long run, that not closing my fifth position would strengthen my technique. To Tumkovsky and Danilova, I appeared lazy, but I could not tell them the reason why I was making this choice. I did not do it to be oppositional, but I did want to get stronger. I wished I could communicate my feelings to them, but I could not. I had to make these choices for myself, even as I kept them secret.

The whole farce was broken when Finis used a picture of me on the front of his Christmas card. He may as well have announced to the world that I was studying with him. My cover was blown, my rebellious double life was compromised. While the teachers at the School of American Ballet likely never came close to seeing that the card, exposing of my secret was the catalyst I needed to make a change. I had to embrace who I was and what I kind of dancer I really wanted to be. I could no longer avoid anyone knowing of the additional training I was receiving and, ultimately, I did not want to. I wanted to immerse myself in these new lessons. I wanted to continue to grow, rather than put effort into pretending I was someone I was not—though it would take many more years of my life, many more experiences both painful and joyful, to fully assemble the puzzle of exactly who that person was.

The deliberate decision to not close my fifth position was a fundamental point in my training, teaching me to not overlook style for substance. Today I do not have a tight fifth position, but I have a clear sense of where to work from, a place to begin movement. A place where I know my center a mind-body connection.

Discovering Balance

I look back on those early days of my dancing life, and I see how out of balance I was. Not physically, not literally. I was practicing the art of physical balance daily in my School of American Ballet courses. I was wearing pointe shoes and learning to balance my entire body weight only on the very tips of my toes. With everything I was learning and practicing, I thought I understood the concept of balance. But to understand balance completely, one must expand one's gaze about the meaning of balance as a whole. We should never forget the extraordinary link between the body and the spirit—to be healthy in one necessitates being healthy in the other. Balance is, of course, a physical component of dance, of movement in general. But balance is also something ineffable, spiritual, that one must find in oneself in order to find peace and purpose in one's life. In dance, balance can appear to be perfect stillness—but it is built of constant, almost invisible movement. It's a negotiation between movement and time, in a way. Balance in life is much the same. I was zeroing in on an idea that is essential to balance, the idea of center, through my work on developing my mind-body connection.

Thinking about balance and about my personal journey to finding balance in dance and in life makes me think about my family. Just as a tree finds balance in a strong system of roots, so too do I find steadiness and balance in understanding my foundations. I will speak of many teachers in this book—those who taught me dance, as well as those who teach alongside me. But it would be foolish to skip over those who are my most primary teachers: my parents. Like a lot of parents, they were consciously trying to impart lessons to me and my sisters as they raised us. But as I look closely at their paths through life, the decisions they made about their own balance or lack thereof, it is clear to me that these perhaps unconscious patterns of theirs were also teachers. We, the children, learned both through their active teachings and also through their example. We were absorbing and negotiating our inherited traits, trying to balance them beside our burgeoning selfhood.

My mother was amazing. She had a brilliant mind—elastic and flexible—and was physically much the same way. She was strong-willed and strong-minded, and without her fierce efforts to make going to dance class and going to school possible, I would not be the dancer, artist, or person I am today. When it came to balance, I think my mother's philosophy is best expressed in this: she deeply believed that people were capable of doing more than one thing with their lives. One could both dance and study law. One could be both happy and successful. One did not have to choose between potentially oppositional ideas, one could find balance between them. But to my mother, balance meant that both paths had to be clear options. She was not a dreamer, not a believer in miracles—she prayed at the altar of rigor and study, not fancies nor the whims of desire nor the arbitrariness of born talent. She was not wanton in her encouragement; her praise was directed to areas where she believed we could actually succeed. There was a deep practicality to her approach.

My mother was not the iconoclastic original her own mother was. My grandmother was an entrepreneur and a character. This woman was way ahead of her time. A vegetarian since the early 1920s, she was deeply committed to physical health, leading exercises for local folks in her Queens neighborhood on Far Rockaway Beach every morning. I am sure her focus on yoga and meditative breathing was a surprise to the community living in eastern Queens at that time, but she was always full of surprises like that. In fact, it was my grandmother who taught me to do a backbend one afternoon in her apartment. If I close my eyes, I can almost still feel her soft hand on my back, guiding me, and the soft pile of her carpet meeting my hands. How many grandmothers teach their granddaughters to do that? She was a role model of movement regardless of one's age.

My grandmother spent her time attending lectures on alternative medicine, going to the local synagogue on Friday nights, and shunning visits to the doctor's office. Eventually, she separated from my grandfather, moved to our hometown in New Jersey, and walked everywhere (including to our house, which was a full two miles from hers—all while carrying vegetarian chopped liver to serve for dinner). While my mother was ambitious but realistic, my grandmother found joy in extremes. And while my mother was supportive of my balletic ambitions, my grandmother had some concerns—despite her love of a good backbend.

"These pointe shoes you wear—they're no good, Naomi. I don't like them."

"But—"

"No, I won't discuss it. They'll deform your feet and stunt your growth."

"But look! I can balance on my toes!"

"End of discussion! Here, have some more chopped liver."

I balked at the idea of abandoning my beloved pointe shoes at the time. As a young dancer, it was a privilege to wear pointe shoes; it implied a certain skill, a certain promise of talent. But here I am, no longer a young dancer, but rather a grown woman with a child of my own—and what do I do? I become a vegetarian, just like my grandmother, I raise my son as a vegetarian, too, and I object to pointe shoes for dancers under ten years old.

My grandmother, this woman of extremes, could not have been more different from my grandfather, my mother's father. He was a solemn, well-meaning man, who ran a hardware store in the Bronx. When I think back to him, I see the hardware store almost more clearly than any one feature of his—he was dedicated to that store's success above almost all else. Where my grandmother was wild, he was traditional, focused, single-minded. And there was my mother, situated between them, figuring out who she was and what she believed in between these two very different people. She had to find a balance for herself.

The sense of balance that she discovered and formed in her role as a daughter, however, did not entirely coalesce with her own daughter's. My mother's idea of balance necessitated two equally matched opposites—for my life, that meant dance and school. She did not understand the meaning of diving into a dance career, what a sacrifice that could be. She did not understand what giving up all other desires, such as playing piano for pleasure, might mean to me. For her, the math equation was simple—balance academic obligations with your one great dream. There was no room for commitments that may throw off this core balance. Under these guiding principles, I was never permitted to dawdle at something. Being a dilettante was not an option.

As I grew, the pursuit of other interests fell away. As soon as I did not have the time to practice the piano for one full hour every day, I had to give it up. Same with the flute, the guitar, the violin, voice lessons, and drama classes. All for the study of ballet. Please do not get me wrong—I loved ballet. I still love ballet. But as a young person, exploring the world and discovering myself and my internal joys, I had so many great loves. I loved music. I loved to sing. I loved to perform in more ways than dance alone. Sometimes I daydream about what my life might look like had I continued those pursuits—what other life might have been in store for me. I fantasize about the unconventional work of interdisciplinary artists. I think of radical artistic institutions like the Black Mountain College, an experimental liberal arts college that existed from the 1930s to the late 1950s, dedicated to the belief that art is essential to a full education and cannot be siloed,[1] and I dream about the kind of alchemy that is possible when different sectors of the arts collide inside a single person or place and make something entirely new. Sometimes I wish I had not needed to give up the piano in order to pursue movement; sometimes I think that piano is also movement.

I do not harbor any resentment toward my mother about drawing these hard lines—she was right that all of these pursuits require practice in order to excel. And she believed that excellence was necessary in each realm in order to justify continual study. That was how she created balance in her life—the knowledge that an investment was worth pursuing, that it was worth the time and effort one was committing to it. But I am not only a byproduct of my experiences with my mother. I also have the lessons of my father to balance everything out.

My father accepted my dance classes. He came from a poor family in Chicago, and he liked the fact of his daughter Naomi dancing at such a high level. It brought him joy that one of his daughters could possibly excel in something "erudite" like ballet. For my father, balance was on a more macro scale than it was for my mother. He looked at his three daughters, and he saw us making up a larger, balanced family, all content in our roles. In his mind, Karen, the youngest, was the intellect, I was the dancer, and Lisa, the eldest, was the crafter, with talents like drawing and sewing. He was proud of each of us in those roles. But of course, over time, our roles must change. Different things began to define us—in my father's eyes, and in our eyes. My sister Lisa's diagnosis of scoliosis certainly changed her and my father's relationship. In my memory, it is almost as though he was the one taken the most off-guard by the news. He made it his duty to guide her through daily exercises; he even bought a massage table especially for this task. Lisa would lie face down on that table, mechanically lifting her right arm in time with her left leg, and then lifting her left arm together with her right leg. She and my father would count each repetition in a monotonous drone, over and over again.

I watched as my father and Lisa worked through those exercises and cringed at the joyless effort required. Movement had always been fun for me. Watching how difficult it was to complete these exercises, both physically and psychologically, I drew a line between myself and that workman-like attitude, just as I eventually drew a kind of line between myself and my mother's way of thinking. Watching my father coach Lisa through her exercises and listening to that sad drone of counting taught me that moving should be, and can be, fun. It does not have to feel like a task. I invite you: imagine your brain like a massive library, with endless systems of filing and sorting. If you find movement in the exercise section, then I would advise you to re-shelve it where it belongs—under fun. My other piece of advice? Welcome dilettantism into your life. My mother never allowed it, but I encouraged it. I believe in dabbling. Follow the path of joy. Experiment. If we were only allowed to engage in our personal areas of expertise, we would probably all be miserable. Be a novice. Be a dilettante.

Even as I at times define myself against them, all of these influences—my mother, my father, my sisters, my grandparents—are the roots of my tree. Acknowledging where I come from, where my most primal understandings of the world come from, allows me to see the forces working on me at all times. How to balance joy and effort, how to balance commitment and pleasure: these were life lessons I learned from my family, even as we perhaps ultimately disagree about the best ways to accomplish this. If we look at the concept of balance in dance, however, our philosophies do not disagree. Dance is where our ideas all harmonize. My mother, the balancer of opposites, and my young self, the would-be dilettante, seeking small new experiences all around—we are both right when it comes to balance in movement. Balance is about the push and pull of strong opposites—working with big oppositional forces on a macro level—but it is also about paying attention to the microscopic, acknowledging that it is lots of tiny movements in all different directions that compose a balanced posture, and perhaps a balanced life.

I remember being in a ballet class in New York City as a young person with Gelsey Kirkland, the legendary American ballet dancer, and I watched her work in total awe. She could remain on the tip of her toes in her pointe shoes for what seemed like forever. This is no small feat: to dance en pointe is to support the weight of your entire body on the tips of your fully extended feet with a pointe shoe. As she stood balanced on one foot, Kirkland might have appeared to be perfectly still to the untrained eye—suspended, motionless, in total equilibrium. But as I observed her, I was struck by profound movement within her stillness. Though she held one stance, she was not stationary at all. Rather, she was endlessly creating and re-creating gorgeous positions on the tip of her toe, forever sensing the smallest shifts in her body. Small wavers could be noted as she calibrated and re-calibrated the infinitesimal transferences of her own weight. Observing Kirkland, one could immediately understand a primary principle of balance—that balance is a negotiation, a constant conversation. It is an immediate awareness of finding center, moving away from center, and then moving back again. Balance is not a still position, balance is movement.

In order to achieve balance, we must realize that we are never truly still—our hearts are always beating, our blood always pulsing, the earth always moving. When we stand tall, we can sense the equal and opposite pulls: up and down, side to side, front and back. But most importantly, we acknowledge the up-and-down nature of gravity's effect on us. We imagine the crown of our head moving up toward the sky, while our feet press down into the earth. That is the balance—the activating of the opposition all around us.

Balance is about the awareness of these oppositions as they relate to your own center—balance is found inside your own body, not via some outside support. I often see students rush to practice balance routines, opening their arms out to the sides, looking like a tightrope walker but energetically moving as if to grab hold of someone or something outside of themselves. There is nothing to the side of you to hold onto, nothing outside of yourself will grant you true balance. The center—that middle point of perfect balance—is inside of your own body. It is always circulating, never still. Be aware and conscious of center in an active way. You must move slowly, attentively, following the order of events of balance. Focus on your feelings of movement, not stillness. When you slow down and focus on the sensation, how does your sense of your center change?

Understanding the distribution and energy of equal and opposite pulls of energy was astounding when I first encountered that thought. David Howard first said those words to me when I was taking a class with him at fourteen years old. Originally from England, David had been teaching in the United States since the mid-1960s. He was a brilliant kinesthetic thinker and educator who was not only teaching me and other young people but also teaching preeminent dancers like Mikhail Baryshnikov, Ohad Naharin, and Gelsey Kirkland herself. In hindsight, David totally embodied the idea of equal and opposite. He taught dancers at opposite ends of the professional spectrum with equal rigor and attention. His long, elegant features widened in kindness when he smiled. But as he told me the words "equal and opposite," he felt less like a kindly teacher and more like a sorcerer whispering a magic spell. It was as if a light bulb exploded in my head and rained gentle electrical currents through my body. My whole form became animated in an instant: though, just like Gelsey, I was not moving at all. He conjured "equal and opposite" in me, and I could feel the energy traveling down my body, out of my feet on the floor, at the same time as it traveled up, shooting from the top of my head. To imagine equal and opposing pulls of energy forever changed my understanding of balance. Again, balance was not only active instead of passive, but it was also motion instead of stillness.

Remember: one's leg actually has weight to it. When extending the leg in one direction, you also have to feel the weight of the arm counterbalancing. You have to think and act like a tightrope walker with a pole—the pole clearly has some weight. Think: side to side, front to back, even up and down energy. For dancing, however, the most important sensation is awareness of side to side.

Some of the most creative thinking on balance comes from the world of contact improvisation, an international dance technique invented by Steve Paxton. It is a way of dancing that actively seeks and celebrates moments of unbalance. Paxton defines contact improv as a relaxed and overflowing form of movement that is open and prepared for the unexpected possibilities that spontaneously arise between a dancer and their partner in the midst of improvisation.[2] This includes how they can mutually support one another while dealing with gravity, mass, momentum, and friction. For contact improv, developing a keen knowledge of balance is essential, especially for a form where we do not always know what might happen next. Until a dancer learns all the ins and outs of balance, it can be difficult for them to take risks, embrace the unknown, and learn to respond spontaneously to whatever the present moment might bring.

Like most other dance techniques, contact improvisation associates balance with locating our center. Some dance methodologies imagine the body's center about two or three inches below our belly buttons, but, for contact improvisers, the entire pelvic girdle can become a source of support. This is what we call a strong center or core. Once we become at home with such centering, we are more willing to move beyond its comfort zone. But just how does one go about centering? Contact improvisation has found that one effective tool is the use of imagery. Years later, in San Francisco, my contact improvisation teacher Martin Keogh would encourage us to imagine such fantastic situations as attaching our pelvic girdle to the ground with a tap root, as this would connect us to the very center of our spinning planet. He would ask us to imagine ourselves as an artesian spring surging up from our core or just stand and imagine the earth is breathing us. These simple images helped us grasp how gravity tugs at our bodies, pulling us from below and simultaneously pushing us from above. Martin would say that this put us kinesthetically in the center, giving us a sense of being both supported and held between two forces rather than one.

From here we would move on to one of my favorite exercises that Martin called the Feather and the Boulder. This is a wonderfully simple, straightforward exercise: each member of the class was asked to choose between being either a feather or a boulder. I loved being a boulder since in ballet I was always being told to act like a feather. The image of being a boulder led me to naturally drop my center and move away from my partner. This made me heavier for my partner who had been instructed to lift me up. Then it was my turn to pick up my partner who had decided to be a feather. Feathers tended to raise their centers and put them close to their partner's core, this would make them lighter. Each choice taught us something about the other, and both choices showed us how helpful the imagination can be in understanding the ways balance actually manifests itself in our bodies.

After our time as boulders and feathers, we would move onto a more physically focused exercise called Two Against One. Here two people stood tightly side by side with their arms crossed against their rib cages. They were pitted against a third person, also with their arms crossed, who was tasked with pushing against the fronts of the pair. The pair was tasked with slowly pushing the single person backward so they could feel the very edge of their strength. Meanwhile, the job of the single person was to attempt as best they could to push the pair backward for the same experience. This lesson was about finding ground and center, as well as learning how to be a good pusher. We were also encouraged to grunt which might have been the very first time I ever made a conscious sound while dancing. That alone was something of a revelation. Martin loved to remind us that the word "grunt" shared the same root as words like "ground" and "groin." Now, whenever I think of balance, it is hard for me not to think of these three essential Gs and how they are so intricately connected to one another.

There are several simple exercises that we practice in order to feel balance, and they were inspired by my dedicated student Donna. I first met Donna in a class called Strength Training for Seniors at NYU's Coles Gymnasium. Donna was a regular presence in our sessions, and I had grown to expect seeing her thin frame and cheerful face every week. It was shocking, then, when she stopped showing up. For months, no Donna. But as suddenly as she had disappeared, she was back! We were overjoyed and clamored for updates on her life.

"We've missed you so much in strength training, Donna! Where have you been?"

"Rusk!" she answered with enthusiasm.

". . . Rusk? What's Rusk?" We were confused. Donna explained: she had been spending her time at the Rusk Institute of Rehabilitation Medicine at NYU's Langone Health. Months before, she had started experiencing dizziness and nausea. The diagnosis: benign paroxysmal positional vertigo (BPPV), or loose crystals in her inner ear. Our ears are not just responsible for hearing, but also for our sense of balance. We all have tiny crystals in our ears made of calcium—these crystals help inform our brain of our heads' movement. If the crystals get dislodged from their normal place in our inner ear, we can feel out of balance, or dizzy. That is what had happened to Donna. When confronted with BPPV, Donna dedicated her time to learning rehabilitative exercises from the Rusk Institute focused on improving balance, and they had helped enormously.

"You have to teach me those exercises!" I exclaimed. Donna was happy to oblige, and since then, I have incorporated those movement patterns into my regular teaching practice.[3]

My mother did everything she could to make it possible for me to dance, even negotiating allowances out with the school system so that I could attend for only part of the academic day. Each year, I left school earlier and earlier. First a half an hour early, then an hour, then more and more. Three days a week of dance classes at the School of American Ballet turned into four days, turned into every day. By the time I was in high school, I was going to school only one hour a day. First period was homeroom from 8:00 a.m. to 9:00 a.m., and then I was on the bus to New York City for my 10:00 a.m. ballet class.

Looking back now, I do not know how I did it. Studying before school, barely stepping foot in the building before leaving again. I craved a life with no rational system of balances or checkpoints or grades or deadlines or typical career goals. I wanted to have no traditional professional options at all, I wanted to be a New York City artist. I imagined getting on a bus and plunging headlong into the city, ready to sink or swim. But my mother was an educator, and a determined one at that. College was important. After I was done with this "dance thing," there should be college and a real career lying in wait. And by real career, she meant, lawyer or businesswoman, something salaried, verified, and validated by traditional appearances of American success. Even though I was barely attending school, my mother insisted that I study and take all the necessary steps to apply to college. I was able to prepare and sit for the SAT exams, and I earned my high school diploma one year early, graduating at sixteen.

At last, I was free of the final barrier to a full-time life in dance. I moved into a New York City apartment right next to the School of American Ballet so that I could study all day. Or, rather, as much of the day that was left free outside of work. To afford the apartment and lessons, I got a job as a waitress in a nearby gym that had a café attached. It was great—I served tuna fish salads all day and used their swimming pool and sauna whenever I wanted. In so many ways, my mother and I had done it. I had finished school, and I was following my dream of dancing. But as ever, even the smallest unaccounted for movement can throw one off balance.

When I was not slinging tuna fish sandwiches or dancing, I was hanging out with the boy next door. Brandon was the son of a teacher at the School of American Ballet. Truth be told, I really had a crush on his father, but Brandon was as close as I was going to get. Brandon was gentle. He played me Beatles songs on his guitar. He was very sweet and, compared to me anyway, a little naive. I had a boyfriend in high school, and I was more experienced in matters of romance and sex than Brandon was. I felt very grown up to be teaching him. We had a fun time together, the way sixteen-year-olds might have fun with an empty apartment in between work shifts and dance classes. I thought we were being safe. I was wrong.

I ended up in the hospital, getting an abortion. I never told Brandon. My parents were distraught. Soon after, I left the School of American Ballet. After ten years, I left them confused. Why was I leaving? Where was I going? What had changed? I could not answer, exactly. But with my SAT scores and high school diploma in hand, I applied to every New York City college out there—Barnard College was the first to send me an acceptance letter, and I jumped at it. I would go to Barnard, study English. And I thought I would never dance again.

Balance is not perfect stillness, it is not stasis. It is not a statue frozen in marble, it is not the total adherence to one shape, one path, one moment suspended in time. It is movement from side to side. It is constant motion, adjustment, listening, learning, and changing. Sometimes when we feel off balance, we simply need the smallest adjustment to set us upright again.

Stretching Myself

Gaining Mobility

I leaned my head against the cool glass of the bus window and watched the cars driving alongside us across the George Washington Bridge. I squinted to see who occupied each car. I tried to imagine the details of their lives, their own particularities. I tried to imagine where they were coming from and where they were going. It disheartened me a bit to think that all these people—all these individuals I was traveling alongside—would always be strangers to me. We were all traveling along parallel paths that would never intersect: like the colorful lines on subway maps, side by side but ever separate. I looked around the bus at my fellow travelers: they were all strangers too. These passengers were all closed books to me; they all had stories I would never hear, never know. We were all together here, traveling the same route in the same vehicle, but we were alone. The thought made me sad. But perhaps I was just in a sad mood in general. That day I was traveling from Barnard back home to New Jersey, taking the very same bus that I used to take home from the School of American Ballet. I was traveling along the same road, but it was as though I was a stranger to myself. The girl traveling back from Barnard that day was not the girl who traveled back from the School of American Ballet years earlier. Our paths had diverged—my new life severed me from the person and the dancer I once was. The transition out of a life of ballet can be difficult: one must radically redefine oneself, relearn how to spend one's time. While I was happy at college, being on that same bus, crossing that same bridge, seeing that same landscape blur past me through the window, made me feel detached from myself, alone.

I was wrong about so many things on that bus. I was wrong that everyone on that bus would always and forever be a stranger. Little did I know it, but one of those people would turn out to be my next boyfriend. More than that: he would be a vital part of my journey back to dance. Oh, and he would also be one more thing: the future editor of *The New Yorker*. Oh yes, that handsome young man sitting a few seats in front of me on that bus was David Remnick.

After twenty minutes of talking on that ride to New Jersey, David and I unearthed the following things. First, my father was his mother's neurologist. Second, David believed that women with overbites were more attractive because an overbite draws attention to high cheekbones. Third, David's father was a dentist and, I was pretty sure, the source of this cheekbone theory. David was a junior at a nearby university, but he was taking the year off to live in New York City for six months and then spend the remainder of the year in Paris. We spent those six months dating, writing, dancing, and exploring the city. I was a new English major, but David was already experienced at college-level writing. Needless to say, David Remnick was a gifted writer and editor even then. I would watch him write, and it was as though he was dancing. His mind had mobility, flexibility. It seemed as though he was not holding tight to thought; he let it guide him in its flow. He told me then that he dreamed of writing for the *Village Voice*, his favorite publication at the time. I had absolute faith he would achieve his dreams, and exactly when I needed it most, David believed in my dream too.

For so long, I had believed (or was encouraged to believe) that I was on one path, and to stray from it meant abandoning that path forever. But David did not think like that, and he encouraged me not to think like that either. He embodied a spirit of flexibility, of pliancy, of bending with the curves in the road rather than pulling over the car. He was intrigued by ballet, and he encouraged my reentry into ballet while simultaneously appreciating my new interests in academics, socializing, and pursuing leadership positions at Barnard. He loved to watch me dance with the variety of independent teachers I was training with in New York—it did not matter to him that it was not the prestigious School of American Ballet. Life did not need to look one particular way to David, he could be flexible. And watching him, I learned to be flexible too.

Flexibility can mean lots of different things to lots of different people. Sometimes when people speak of flexibility, they are really speaking of open-mindedness. Keeping one's beliefs and approaches to life limber so that they do not snap when they encounter the first resistance. Flexibility can of course also be physical and literal—the relative stiffness of the muscles, the ability of the body to move and stretch and bend. Ironically, this kind of flexibility is often an area where people, and new dancers especially, get very inflexible in their judgments about themselves and what they are capable of. People think you have to be flexible in order to dance, rather than understanding that flexibility is not a prerequisite to moving. Instead, flexibility changes and grows through movement.

When I told my younger sister, Karen, that I was working on this book, she immediately asked me why she was not in it. Karen prefers to exercise her brain rather than her body. She is a scientist, a renowned chemist, teaching and conducting research on finding new energy solutions at a university. I am envious of her quick mind, easily understanding any problem—except how, when, and how much to move. My brain and body were set in one way, and hers in another. To me, we have always been that way. But as we began this conversation recently, she revealed something to me that made me question my own inflexibility in my assumptions about myself and my sister. She confessed to me at that moment that dance training as a young person had been denied her. When she auditioned for the School of American Ballet, she was rejected because of her lack of flexibility. That experience had a lifelong impact on her attitude toward dance. She felt that dancing had rejected her, so she rejected dance. All of this was new to me, it was not how I remembered our childhood. But Karen remembered, in vivid detail, sitting while we were playing jacks and not being able to spread her legs like me in a V position. All of this was heartbreaking for me to hear—so much of my practice now is about encouraging people who feel cut off from their own mobility and flexibility, and I was discovering that I had not been able to help my own sister with those same problems. I cast my mind back to sitting on the floor, playing jacks, and I can think of so many positions that Karen could sit in that would stretch her legs and would increase her flexibility. The open V position is not the only position that encourages a stretch. Now I know how many other positions are possible, but the challenge of not being able to find those positions for herself impacted Karen's mobility.

Unfortunately, this is a fairly common story. Many people tell themselves or are told by others, "You can't dance, you're not flexible." Flexibility and dance seem inextricably linked in people's imagination, but somehow our imaginations are not facile enough to allow for other kinds of flexibility, other choices to make with one's body. This search for choices, for new ways of being in one's own body, is a tenet of my work. It is a purposeful rejection of the traditional rules of how to sit, stand, stretch. As a child, I felt conflicted for being the dancer in the family, but Karen presented me with the challenge of finding a way to dance for all bodies in a very personal way.

It is essential that we rethink what we think we know about dance—so often we are inheriting previous ideas rather than asking ourselves to think outside our personal boxes. Many of my fundamental experiences of dance come from ballet, because that is the movement I gravitated toward naturally as a young person more than jazz or modern techniques. I craved the kind of lyric movement ballet asked of a dancer; I craved the sense of reaching toward something illusive, the encounter between a real body and its limitations and the sense of moving beyond those limitations. As a young dancer, I was never very comfortable with jazz technique. Too much energy, I thought at the time, too much of a show. I could not see what jazz technique really was—I was distracted by what I saw as theatricality, artificiality, and a showiness that did not feel, to me, like it was coming from the truth of the body. My mind was stubbornly inflexible when it came to what that mode of movement could offer. But the best lessons can come from places you do not expect. A significant turning point in my own understanding of mobility came not from ballet, but instead from a dancer trained in jazz technique.

I have come to recognize jazz dance as one of the quintessential American art forms. There are multiple meanings and styles of jazz dance, and its improvisatory spirit has become an integral part of the culture of our nation. Jazz has its roots in West African culture, which was brought to the United States by enslaved Africans through the transatlantic slave trade. Scholar Sheron Wray identifies four Africanist aesthetics that are the principles of jazz dance: rhythmicity, improvisation, dynamic play, and a relationship with the music. In the United States, the roots of jazz were influenced by the mixing of Africans from different tribes and cultures, restrictions on the dance and musical practices of enslaved peoples, and the incorporation of some European-based movements. Many historians agree that jazz as a musical form was likely born in New Orleans in the early twentieth century, and the term "jazz dance" was coined in the 1920s, when dances like the Lindy Hop and the Charleston gained popularity.

The irrepressible style and inspiration of jazz dance spread to the worlds of Broadway and Hollywood throughout the twenty-first century, making jazz one of our country's most beloved dance forms.[1]

Jazz remains, to this day, an infectious celebration of exuberance, individuality, virtuosity, and spontaneity. It starts in your foot. Your whole foot. Then shifts to the other. Each time, taking on the full weight of your body. Left then right, then left again. Full foot. Full weight. Let the ground become a drum and bang that rhythm out with your feet. Once it starts, it is hard to stop. It moves from feet to legs, from legs to hips. Each body part is slowly liberated in what jazz dancers call moments of isolation. This allows a body part to freely articulate itself. It is as if you were re-animating your body, body part by body part. Hips then ribcage. Something was missing, I was lost, and it was jazz that became the bridge from the rarified world of Lincoln Center to the downtown hipster chic of Soho.

"Let it go!" the jazz instructor said. "Let what go?" I thought. I was in rehearsal for a new play, and the choreography asked for a specific side-to-side motion that I was struggling with. I felt stuck. I had no idea how to "loosen up." I was not activating my pelvis in the right way, and I knew it. He pointed to my behind and told me again, "Let. It. Go." The muscle he was referring to was the gluteus maximus, the main extensor muscle of the hip. And there it was: I did not know where to move from. I needed to "let go" of certain muscles in order to allow other muscle groups to move. A radical thought! In order to slide the pelvis from side to side, up and down, I needed to figure out how to let go of the held muscles in my glutes which I had used for years to stand erect in the form of ballet. I had been engaging with the sense of the vertical, "pulling up." But here, I had to study "release." I had to release the muscle of the glutes, literally "let go" of my glutes, my rear end. At the same time, I had to understand how to stand up in the new way with loose hips, supported by my core. While ballet is a core tenet of my dancing life and dancing practice, it did not teach me the entire gamut of movement. I could continue exploring the muscles literally keeping me erect, continue exploring my lower abdominals, and play with letting things go rather than holding them tight.

This jazz dancer, with his "Let it go!" mantra, invited me to access more movement. Dance grants you the ability to be more facile, to bend, to stretch, to move quickly while moving safely. But, perhaps counter-intuitively, you have to find a way to release muscles in order to move more quickly, rather than really work or strain your muscles. When your muscles are tight, when you do not let it go, you cannot be as clear in your direction, as a dancer or as a person simply moving through the world. When we speak about mobility, we are talking about moving in a loose manner with seemingly little muscle strength. We could also call this moving from the bones.

There is an idea that if the bones line up, you only have to follow that progression in order to achieve the movement combination—in dance, and in quotidian movement. What we are after is a way to get the bones to line up properly, evenly, without pulling to one side and using muscle strength to achieve the movement. Habits of life have moved us sideways, tilted our heads in one direction, our knees another, our shoulders lifted, our pelvis forward (etc.). These unique variations are what give us special-ness, and we will return to these physical imprints of life and their poten-tial in dance in later chapters. But as we build our physical understand-ing through the mind-body connection and a balanced relationship with our center, we are also going to work on relaxing our body, relaxing our muscles, in order to move freely and move from an aligned place. Some of this work is influenced by jazz movements—the sway of the hips, the isolations, the swing of the pelvis.[2]

During those early years at Barnard, I reconnected with my own flexibil-ity in many ways. I was relearning how to be in a romantic relationship. I would eventually rediscover dance—on different terms, with different teachers, who exposed me to different and new ideas. And it was there, at Barnard, that I began to understand leadership, community, and how to work in a group—an act of flexibility if there ever was one.

My first year at college, I was elected Officer of the Board of Barnard College's Student Government. This was my first experience as a leader, but more importantly, it was an opportunity to connect with other like-minded students at Barnard, even if perhaps we did not seem so alike from the surface. This was a new experience for me. I had come from a world of homogeny—slim, white ballerinas, all vying to be seen as better than the other. Now at Barnard, I needed to open my eyes to new ways of thinking, new ways of relating to a cohort of women. As an Officer, I was introduced to women of different sizes, shapes, and attitudes. I met Marcia

Sells, from Detroit. She was a dancer too—she had trained at the Dance Theatre of Harlem. She was a ballerina who later became a lawyer and now, a Barnard Trustee. She was in my first piece of choreography, created as part of a production of *The Winter's Tale* with the Columbia Players..

Within and among this community, I not only became a better dancer, I became a leader. I discovered the power of choice, confidence, and leadership at Barnard that very first year. We planned activities together, created postings of those activities, integrated with faculty and other students, learned the workings of advocacy and its results. I ended my first year of college understanding how policies worked and gaining the courage to be a voice for change. By the end of my time at Barnard I had been transformed into a leader, a choreographer, and an artist. My senior thesis was a piece of my own choreographing. Even then, I knew this choreographic creation was a culmination and celebration of all the people I had met at Barnard, the art that excited me and the community I had formed. The work was staged around a six-foot tall wooden triangle, with twelve dancers, one of whom was June Omura, who later became a dancer with Mark Morris's company, and changed the landscape of dance in New Paltz, New York. I wrote the spoken text myself; and we used new musical compositions by Marianne Weems on electric violin, who later became the artistic director of an avant-garde company. The dance itself was inspired by the physical gesture of leaning, and it told the story of how we lean on others to achieve, how we move forward through partnerships. It was a distillation of everything Barnard taught me. I was outstretching my creative mind to include new interdisciplinary concepts and collaborators, new forms, new radical music. I was building things with people entirely different from me, but with whom I could be flexible enough to respond to their new ideas and contributions. I named the piece *How to Live on Slope*. One cannot simply fall down when life gets hard. One must live in communion with others. One must think of a new way.

I had come to Barnard as though emerging from a cocoon. Everything in my life had been pointing toward dance, toward the School of American Ballet for so long, that dropping out felt like failing, like I had lost my chance at happiness, at a meaningful life. But I did not stay stuck in that way of thinking, I moved past it. I kept my mind limber, kept my imagination for my life open and pliable. Staying flexible about who you are and what you might be able to do is not just a key to dance, but a key to life. But just as movement becomes easier, more fluid, when you line up your bones, so too does life start to become easier when you are in line with your own purpose. I look back on this time, and it is clear to me that I was aligned with my ultimate purpose: to dance, to collaborate, to choreograph, to put community forward, and to lead.

Growing in Strength

Building strength is about repetition, commitment, and discipline—but in my life, building strength is also about embracing serendipity. Perhaps that may seem strange, but I have found that the natural, ineffable, mysterious path of your life is actually leading you toward honing your skills, building your muscles, and building physical memory. Building strength can be a matter of spending time in a gym, or it can also be living your life in a way that is physically aware, and physically engaging.

In the summer of 1983, I studied how to work strength-building into my routine as a new modern dancer. Beginning my senior year at Barnard College and having struggled with one year of modern dance, I realized dance was completely in my life but I still was not certain about how to dance healthily and holistically. I thought building upper body strength would improve that study. Ballet had torqued my thinking about strength for most of life—I had always emphasized strength in the lower body but had not occupied my thoughts as much with my arms and chest. I wanted to formally build upper body strength. My brilliant idea was to do this by working the fishing boats in Alaska. I planned to head out west to hoist salmon, conveniently building upper body strength at the same time.

Traveling west with the objective of getting to be a strong modern dancer was the ultimate goal. I knew the daughter of a college friend whose family lived on a farm in Idaho. As good a place to start as any. Also, there was a dance community of contact improvisers who lived in Boise, and I could start my journey to Alaska from there.

But in Boise I quickly learned about farming, and living with cows and on farmland was a challenge enough. The fishing boats would have to wait; they did sound dangerous, the more I thought about it. Farm work required serious upper body strength. While staying with the family, my job was to track and feed the cows. After chores, I could wander through the town of Boise and dance in a modest studio. The people who built the studio were a husband and wife team, who invited me to explore the woods and trails in the nearby Boise forests with them. In addition to my time dancing, we would hike through the riverbeds together in the afternoons. I thought this was most exotic: it was an activity that required an ability to both sense where to move along with a constant balance challenge. I got very skilled at picking paths at a quick speed and avoiding tumbling over rocks, getting wet, or missing steps—not unlike the challenge of a double turn en pointe. I thrived being challenged by this kind of clear objective: staying upright and using my upper body to counterbalance my weight, in the rhythm of taking steps, with speed. I loved rock climbing and being in nature. I loved the cows, the fields, and hauling pails of milk. I grew strong in a natural way, meeting my original objective. Many years later, when choreographing a dance and working with a group of women who lived on Martha's Vineyard, I could appreciate their sense of their own upper bodies from having lived so much of their lives close to nature. They walked on the beach and in fields, had dogs, gardened the earth; they were very different from the older dancers in NYC, because their lives were different. They could get up and down from the floor; they were comfortable using their own body weight. They understood how to be in nature, how to engage their bodies in a more connected way when doing their daily activities, and while exercising and dancing. I could appreciate this and used their ability as an asset in our work together. Upper body strength, as well as developing a sound connection of balance between the upper and lower body, was simply a way of life for these dancers: a reinforcement of the lessons I learned so many summers ago in Boise.

All this led me to realize that when we think of strength, we often think about it in the general sense of "I can lift this" or "I can endure that." But the real question is, what are you lifting or enduring? Every task usually requires a different kind of strength, and that strength usually comes from an entirely different way of working with our bodies. This is also true of dance, where different schools of movement demand different kinds of strength, and this can ultimately lead to different kinds of training. What if you, like contemporary American choreographer Elizabeth Streb, want to fly—all on your own, without the aid of another ballet dancer throwing you up in the air? How does one go about strengthening themselves to become the dance equivalent of an action hero? If you want to fly on your own and land safely, then there can be no weakness in your joints, ligaments, tendons, or muscles. You are going to have to be as strong on the bottom of your body (hips and legs) as you are on top (gut, torso, and arms). In other words, your body is going to end up looking more like a trapeze artist than a prima ballerina, because the job requirement of flying all on your own demands a completely different kind of strength.

In Streb's world this means following the regimen of certain high-wire performers whose average week begins with a hundred push-ups a day, jumping rope, lifting weights, and even boxing whenever they get a chance. Why boxing? Because it is good for a trapeze artist's reflexes, preparing them for those inevitably unexpected blows to the face, shoulders, or chest when they accidentally collide in midair with their partner and are forced to think fast. As a result of such strength training, a Streb dancer will not likely decline an outrageous feat of virtuosic physicality, but rather strategize about the muscles that need to be developed first. For Streb, it is all about the muscles. She will say, "Our muscles drag our skeleton around."[1] If we just strengthen those muscles, we can take that skeleton to places it never dreamed of being, like midair. The only things stopping us are certain narrow-minded perceptions that have surrounded the use of our bodies since childhood, habits of thought that are often difficult to notice, let alone change. Streb has spent a lifetime addressing these misconceptions, one muscle group at a time. She still believes, to this day, that human flight and its pursuit is a reasonable goal, and watching her dancers whirl about above our heads, you cannot help but think: she just might be right. Perhaps all it will take is just one more push-up.[2]

After my summer in Boise I returned to Barnard, graduated, and promptly set out west again. I was like a magnet to the West Coast, and I found myself living and working in San Francisco. Working as a ballerina at the San Francisco Ballet? Not quite. Rather, I was working my first full-time job as an assistant in accounts payable at an advertising agency. As one can guess, accounts payable was not the most physically engaging field. I had limited time during my day to move my body. During lunch break I encouraged my coworkers to move themselves, and we created a regular lunchtime routine of dancing exercises. Besides that, the hours that were available to me were the early morning before heading to the office, and then in the evening after work, which were hours I wanted to dedicate to rehearsals and performances. I was initially unsure how to acclimate my body to the change in lifestyle; namely, the shift from moving all day, staying limber, and remaining ever-ready to dance, to sitting at a desk and remaining largely stationary from 9 to 5. However, my boyfriend at the time, Peter, introduced me to weight training. He and I would work out together starting at 6:00 a.m. at the YMCA in downtown San Francisco, and then afterward head in for a full day of office work. He taught me all about the machines and how to use them.

The year I spent building muscle at the YMCA was inspiring for many reasons: I learned the importance of feeling your muscles grow by breaking down and recovering muscle, and how to achieve that growth practically and quickly. Through experimentation, I discovered which machines had the maximal impact—I looked to the assisted pull-up machine, for example, to activate both the primary muscles, an important group of deltoids and pectorals, and the secondary muscles of the abdominals and latissimus dorsi. Even with the difficulties of my schedule, or perhaps because of it, I realized the importance of consistent workouts as opposed to sporadic sessions to achieve long-term health. Eventually I understood and delighted in changing up the workout routines in order to promote muscle strengthening. As a result of the patient teachings of my then-boyfriend Peter and other experts who instructed me on correct form and use, I began to feel at home in a gym.

I could not have known in 1983 how essential my experience in Boise would be for future dance projects, and I could not have known in 1984 how vital that weight-training experience would be for my future life as a teacher. But just as our habits of life shape our physical being, so too do they seem to shape the course of our lives. I never planned on knowing my way around a gym, on gaining a knowledge of weight training and strengthening, but it was fortunate I had—it served me immeasurably when in 1993, a decade later, I found myself working as a fitness instructor for seniors in New York City. Because of the home I had carved out for myself in that gym in San Francisco, I was able to clearly explain the benefits and methods of strengthening exercises and was therefore uniquely situated to develop approaches for the older adults in my courses to strengthen their bodies.

Later in life, when I returned to New York City, I studied senior fitness in order to understand more deeply the major muscle groups impacted by age, and adapted the knowledge set I had acquired in the 1980s to best serve my students. I was blessed with longtime colleague Lisa, who had taught the class for years before and had enormous stores of experience to impart. She was not a dancer, however, and I was. That was where my conception of the body truly began, and if I was to be the instructor, that would be how my students also accessed their strength within their bodies. I would tell them they were dancers and to behave that way, imbuing their movements with a dancer's alignment and grace.

While teaching strength training for seniors in New York City, I met Matilda. Approximately sixty-five years old at the time, Matilda was slender and awkward but striking in her stature with long, elegant fingers. Her powerful presence made me notice her right away, but equally noticeable was the cane she used in order to walk into the gym. Despite the cane, she performed the weight exercises, week after week. She hardly increased weight levels, but she was steadily increasing repetitions. I always ask students for regularity rather than effortful pushing with an exercise. As Matilda worked, over time, minuscule changes were starting to appear in her physicality. One day, she began to leave the cane on the side of the room and perform the exercises while moving freely from machine to machine. She was gradually getting stronger.

It was amazing to watch Matilda grow in strength and confidence—and in turn, her new power gave me renewed strength and confidence as a teacher. It is one thing to know how dance has affected your own life, but it is another entirely to witness its impact on others. Matilda became an invaluable champion of my work—eventually becoming not only a regular student but an important adviser and board chair of my dance company. Matilda continued to take classes with me of all kinds, moving from strength training to classes focused around dance. She valued the lessons movement taught her about health, so much so that she started her own health-focused meetup with other students from my classes. She arranged gatherings before our class time for like-minded people to discuss better health solutions around diet and regular exercise. Welcoming my students into class after their meetings with Matilda was a gift. Everyone was so inspired to move, to choose health, and to think of themselves as powerful agents in their lives as their bodies changed with age.

One day, I watched Matilda as she walked across the room. "Pick up your feet from the floor," I told her, not thinking much of it. This seemed a simple enough idea to me at the time. Matilda later told me, however, that this phrase had become her mantra as she walked. She then wisely asked me if, in my teaching, this concept was something I could consciously choose to teach to more people, something I could encourage my older students to think about and employ daily. It was a simple request, but it was also revolutionary. I had not understood how truly important the concept of lifting one's feet was for older bodies and those with challenged mobility—it felt so natural to my body then. But this idea cannot be underestimated: it is critical to remember to pick your feet up. This is of course true for dance, but even more true for quotidian actions like walking, in order to avoid tripping and prevent falls. Take larger steps! Don't shuffle! What I did not realize until purposefully teaching that principle, as Matilda suggested, is this: it is one thing to know in your mind that you should pick up your feet, it is another to actually have the strength and skill to accomplish it. Both the thought and the strength to follow through on the thought are necessary. Both require time and practice.[3]

These exercises were instrumental for developing Matilda's strength. During the winter break of that year, when I started dance classes for this group of seniors, she was one of the key members. She was able to see clearly how the effort of moving with mindfulness enabled her to think of herself with a dancer's awareness of form and be able to improvise.

Matilda passed in 2014 after an issue with her aorta; her heart was not pumping the needed blood to function. When we first met, I had been struck by her impressive height—I later learned that trait was linked to Matilda's Marfan syndrome, a condition that accelerated her growth beyond the usual parameters. Her heart problems were a result of this genetic condition that can cause death by age forty. Like most genetic conditions, the person affected needs to maintain health measures in order to prolong life. Matilda told me that practicing dance was one of the things that kept her going, that prolonged her life. She was an inspiration to me as a teacher and to the other students. I will always remember her telling me that I was the first one who told her to pick up her feet when walking. I met her when she was sixty-five years old, already twenty years older than her life expectancy predicted. She passed fifteen years later, having successfully transitioned from walking with a cane to dancing without. Her influence remains alive in my life, and alive within this book; she was not only exemplary in her strength-building, but also her expressiveness as a dancer.

The Space We're In

To introduce you to another fundamental of movement, let me take you back to California and introduce you to another devoted dance teacher, David Nillo. I wish you could meet David the way I met him: picture in your mind's eye a gymnasium. Just an ordinary gymnasium. Imagine the shiny wooden floor, the basketball hoops, the colorful lines demarcating space on the floor. Maybe it seems like nothing special, at first: we could be in any YMCA. But the more you look around, the more you are shocked by the vastness of the space. The space seems to double and triple before you—and in fact it does, holding enough room for three basketball courts. But even though the space is large and cavernous, it does not feel empty. Perhaps now you sense a twinkle of something magical—you hear the hint of a laugh, maybe. And then the answer comes to you. The entire space crackles with joy. Suddenly, music bursts into the space. You see a pair of people moving across the floor. And then another. And another. They glide—or hop! or spin!—in a diagonal line from one end of the gym, across the expanse, to the opposite end. You perceive colors—the pink of soft, silk ballet shoes, but also the bright yellow and red of a running sneaker, the gleam of tennis whites, the shock of neon-green athletic shorts, the cool, deep, tight black of a leotard, perfectly complementing the soft elephant-gray of sweatpants. Two by two by two, pair after pair, pas de bourrée and arabesques, each couple dances along the diagonal, each occupying their slice of space, visible in the vast space, colorful and distinct as tropical birds.

And there, at the helm, was David. Handsome, still boyish somehow, despite being in his seventies, with well-worn laugh lines around his eyes and a kind of lift in his eyebrows, like he was always ready to be in on a joke. Commanding the room with equal parts humor and technical rigor. Imagine thinking to yourself: How is he doing this? How are all these different people here? What magic draws them here? It's decided: this man will be my mentor.

The scene I just described took place while I was teaching a multi-method modern dance class for adults at the Hollywood YMCA. At that same time, David was also teaching at the Hollywood YMCA. His course was a very popular adult dance fitness class. I discovered that David had a ballet background, like me. He had been a founding member of the original American Ballet Theater, so his knowledge of ballet was impeccable, but he was equally well-versed (and serious about) how to do a simple waltz or the more complicated Susie-Q. His style as a teacher was similarly open and welcoming. Immediately, I was amazed by his ability to connect to his students of all ages, shapes, and sizes. He taught former members of the Martha Graham New York company, Hollywood dancers from the early black-and-white films, tennis-player men in whites and sweats, moms, young adults in the Hollywood scene seeking dance information, and folks who just wanted to socialize at the gym class. He honestly believed everyone could master the steps. The students were focused on correct footwork, correct port de bras, correct musicality, and having fun. So much of his class laid the groundwork for Movement Speaks: David taught me that the basics of dance were important and fun. Dance had the power to connect people across communities—from different spaces, he brought them into one. He knew that people wanted to laugh as well as move with ease, and he encouraged different personalities even as he prompted everyone to stand straight. I loved that he kept the music going even during the water break halfway through the session. Even though the class itself was pausing, the energy never dissipated from the room. The song kept moving through your body, your spirit stayed upbeat and alert. With David, your toes were always tapping and your heart always singing—the momentum never lagged. David was wide-ranging in his musical tastes. Show tunes, folksy classical melodies, and familiar opera arias all graced his classes in equal measure. He chose tunes we mostly knew. I learned the power of introducing familiar music, songs that made you want to move, rhythms that got into the body and made smiles bloom involuntarily.

David had a vision of dance for all. In that gymnasium, he created space for everyone: space to move, to dance, to be seen. To dance, a person must possess an inner knowledge of the workings within her own body, but a person also must possess an awareness of all the space around the body— how much space she takes up, what kind of space he may need in order to move freely. I think of David and that gymnasium in every space I choose. Once his class had to move to a dance studio instead of the basketball court, something was lost, actually. Even though the dance studio had all the right equipment—mirrors, a sprung floor—it lacked the magic, the spirit, the freedom of that ordinary gymnasium. We must always be attentive to the space around us.

To a dancer, space means several things. There is the physical, architectural space you are occupying—a gym, a stage, a studio, the steps of a museum—then there is the space your own body takes up within that overall area, and finally there is the spatial relationship you have to the other dancers or other objects present within that architecture. We call this relationship proprioception.

Proprioception, put simply, is how we know where we are in space. It is as significant as sight, smell, taste, touch, and hearing in terms of how we understand our surroundings, and it can be as intuitive. If you were to close your eyes, you would still intuitively know where your limbs are, the rate at which they are moving, where you are directing them. To translate this sensation into the area beyond yourself and gain awareness of how much space you need to move in is profound and life-changing—in fact, the awareness of proprioception is often a tool developed in physical therapy. Dancers, however, are already familiar with this tool, as they develop that sense in their dance practice. This exercise can help those new to dance as well. As you move, you wordlessly, almost unconsciously, ask yourself: How long do I extend my leg? What is the distance between my foot and the floor? What is the width of my reach? Am I tilting too dramatically? How much space do I need between me and the other dancers and the edge of the room? Am I going to run into that other dancer approaching me?

"You're going to run into that other dancer approaching you!" I mentally hissed at myself as I leapt toward the edge of the stage. It was Christmastime, the music was transcendently moving, fake snow fell gently to the stage floor like magic . . . and I was wearing an enormous headpiece that felt three feet tall and a white tutu with what seemed to be an unfairly large circumference. And I was panicking.

If proprioception is how we know where we are in space, then let me situate you in time. This story takes place at the Pacific Northwest Ballet, during a performance of Tchaikovsky's *The Nutcracker*. I had been invited to the Pacific Northwest Ballet as a direct result of the outside-of-school dancing I had studied while at Barnard College. Two directors from the Pacific Northwest Ballet were looking for Balanchine-trained dancers to perform in Balanchine repertoire at their company—and had held auditions at the School of American Ballet. They saw me and offered me the job, so I moved to Seattle to dance with Pacific Northwest Ballet. My first role, my very first time on stage with the company, was stepping in last minute for a dancer as Snow in the company's production of *The Nutcracker*.

If you are unfamiliar with this particular dance from *The Nutcracker*, imagine a small section of sky during a gentle snowfall. Think about how a gust of wind stirs up the flakes—how it creates swirling patterns, how swiftly the wind moves the snowflakes and spins them, yet they never collide. Now imagine that instead of snow moving over a patch of sky, those snowflakes are dancers moving across a stage. Quickly flitting between each other, floating on the air, swirling around each other without ever colliding. Or at least, that is the goal. But how was I to know how big my head was with this headpiece on? It felt huge, like it did not end at all, just kept climbing and climbing. "This is not what heads are supposed to feel like!" I wanted to shout to the other dancers, but they were moving by me too quickly. Entering the stage, exiting the stage, leaping through a sea of white tulle moving in all directions: I was lost, completely turned around. Miraculously I ended up following directions from another dancer and somehow got through the performance without accidentally body-checking anyone and turning the ballet into something more akin to a game of ice hockey. Needless to say, when I looked to the rehearsal board after the performance, my name had been crossed off all future performances of *The Nutcracker*, but it had been a master class in proprioception.

Moreover, it was a profound lesson in the way that our body maps onto our state of mind. To be honest, during that performance I had been unsure of more than just the precise entrances and exits and the height of my headpiece. I was unsure of my body. I was frightened by my power. All I desired was invisibility, to erase myself from the stage. I wanted to look into the eyes of the audience and see nothingness reflected back at me. Ultimately, that performance and that time in my life found me depressed about my future. My relationship to space was inextricably linked to my relationship to taking up space. To being present fully, and to being seen. Thinking deeply about—and improving your relationship to—proprioception can be a personal manifesto about how to live and move freely.

When I think about space, I cannot help but think of the great Merce Cunningham, who revolutionized the whole idea of how dancers related to it. When I first saw a piece by Cunningham and his dancers, I could not find the right word for what I felt. I was filled with a sense of wonder, but also surprise. I was shocked as I watched Cunningham's dancers scattered across the stage space and moving in all directions with no seeming order or unified directionality. Where were the familiar lines, the patterns, the golden triangles that usually organize the space of classical and modern dance? Where was I supposed to look? Who was I supposed to follow? And why were all the dancers not crashing into one another without the usual compositional guardrails? It was as if Cunningham had exploded the stage and the dancers were the moving shards of this massive choreographic detonation. Later, I would learn, that there was a method to this seeming madness. A desire to show dancers and audiences that theatrical space is not one-directional but alive with multiple points of directionality that included our left, right, and back. This was also true of the very space of the dancers' bodies whose arms and legs could also be moving in different directions at the same time. These multiple points in space refused to accept one fixed front, which had traditionally been oriented to wherever the audience was situated. In Cunningham's dance universe, front was wherever the dancer was facing. Cunningham would always say to his dancers: think of yourself moving away from yourself in a direction, and when you get there, well . . . there you are! This opened the dancers up to multiple directions in space, going against hundreds of years of theatrical thinking. You could say Cunningham was the Einstein of dance, shattering old notions and introducing us to a brave new world in the time/space continuum of the stage. In fact, Cunningham had completely embraced Einstein's observations that there are no fixed points in space. This led to one of my all-time favorite quotes from Merce Cunningham: "Center Stage is wherever I am."[1] I think, this may be the greatest piece of advice that any dancer can ever receive.

Let's talk about how to improve our relationship to proprioception. What are the tools that can help develop an awareness of spatial relations? Maybe you are not like me as a dancing snowflake in the Pacific Northwest, wanting to disappear—maybe you are more like my student Nora, who had similar proprioceptive challenges. Nora, an older woman who came to many weekly classes, danced with a sense of largeness that was beyond her body. Other students commented that they did not want to stand too close to her as they felt her swinging arms and awkward excessively large steps would tumble them. She always tended toward the front during performances, eating up the space with enthusiasm. Telling her to watch out for others was not helpful. She did not seem to understand how much room she was taking up. Nora reminded me a bit of Goldilocks and the Three Bears. To me, Goldilocks always seemed a little proprioceptively challenged. She has a hard time figuring out what is too small, what is too large, and what is just right: she spends the story trying to find the right fit for herself. Goldilocks did not have an intuitive understanding of what the right space was for her, just like Nora. Dancers must have a clear understanding of how much space they take up: not too small, not too large, we are looking for the just right. Whenever we are proprioceptively lost, like Nora, we are forgetting the reality of our bodies.

Proprioception is something you can begin to explore imaginatively, even before you start exploring it physically. From where you sit now, begin to bring awareness to your body. Where are you in space? Where are you positioned in the room? How much of that space does your body take up? Wiggle your toes, see if you can stretch your legs. Explore your limits, the edges of your body and your awareness, from your current position. Can you envision the maximum width of your wingspan, the full elongation of your legs? Let your imagination project your body into the space around you. Taking on this sense of projection is owning your body as a dancer. For more ways to creatively distill the concept of proprioception, see the exercises beginning on page 167.

In a way, by examining proprioception, we are also returning to our core fundamental, the mind-body connection. We are understanding how we look on the outside and how we feel on the inside, and then projecting that somatic understanding onto the space around us, outside of us. Part of dance, of movement, is not moving at all but rather is visualizing. Projecting yourself into the space in front of you, predicting where you will move and accomplishing that movement, made all the clearer by the image of it in your mind. In class with Nora, we practiced the idea of general space with the definition of being evenly divided, creating a place for all. The phrase "pepperoni on a pizza" allowed all to understand equal space. All we needed was a visual, an image we could all instinctively picture and re-create with our bodies. It got to the point where I could just say "pepperoni" and all older dancers understood just how far apart they could dance. In order to dance, or even more simply, in order to move thoughtfully and purposefully, we need to project both an understanding deep inward, to our muscles and tendons and ligaments, and project an understanding expansively outward, visualizing ourselves and others in the larger world. That understanding can be felt by anyone. Every person can own that kind of visualization and that kind of visibility.

The word "visibility" immediately returns me to that first day in David's class in the Hollywood YMCA. As I watched each pair cross the floor, the thing that surprised me most, more than the colorful clothing and the diverse collection of people, was the satisfaction radiating from each of the students as they performed in this way. Only a few simple steps before what you could barely call an audience, yet there was a sense of performance of joy and pride. This joy is connected to proprioception. When you alter your relationship with space, when a small group becomes separate from the full group, a performance is created. And though that can be vulnerable and frightening to some at first, especially those that do not see themselves as performers, no one in David's class shied away. It was somehow miraculous, to see a person crossing the room, dancing, full out, speaking clearly but wordlessly of their individual need to be seen. This is the power of a simple step, a combination so associated with the essence of dance, yet filled to the brim with this individual's personality. It did not matter if they were "good" or not. All that mattered was each had a partner and were crossing the space, going across the floor. This combination of proprioception and visibility is a typical exercise in a dance class, and yet it was made so wondrous by the older adults of all shapes and sizes performing in it.

If we were in one of my classes together now, we would begin with a simple traveling pattern and progress to more complicated movements challenged by rhythms. Teachers lead different groups across the floor. We start with a simple walk in time with the music, nothing more. Then the next time we cross the floor, we change the pattern to walking while looking side to side, turning the head. Maybe next time we cross, we walk in beats, step together, step touch to one side and then the other. We progress to hops across the floor, or extensions to step lifts with the front leg on the ball of the foot with the back leg extended behind in an arabesque. Some of the favorite exercises are step touch across the floor with different arm variations, step lift using tilts, slide with legs and arms extended using swinging arms crossing in front of the chest and extending to the sides, simple traveling battements to the front. People enjoy the cardio workout as well as the challenge for balance and mobility. The need for traveling with ease is powerful, and the need to be alongside one other person or with a group at the same time is equally huge. Occupying the space behind your partner, you may think you are not visible. You are still seen, however—there is no way to avoid being seen!

I believe that this relationship between proprioception and visibility—necessary for dancers and non-dancers alike—is best taught and strengthened through dance practice. Through stretching, dance shows you how much room you take up, where your body parts are, how much you extend in space. Through movements like crossing the floor with a partner, like I first saw in David's class in Hollywood, dance instructs you how far you need to travel to get where you want to go. Proprioception is a lesson learned from studying dance but is as valuable a sense as the five senses. It is an essential tool in understanding partnerships, social contracts in life spaces, comfortable distancing between people whether it is with one other person or a group, what feels right in time and space.

The era of COVID-19 affected everyone in the world in myriad different ways, including older adults. The way older adults occupied space drastically changed—in the US, where the isolation of older adults is already an issue, people grew increasingly isolated to protect themselves from illness. That changed their understanding of space, and their relationships to boldly inhabiting it. Dance had never been more valuable from a social or physical perspective. No matter the space we are in, whether we share physical space together or virtual space; whether we are in a studio or an open field or in our own living rooms; we cannot underestimate the need to create space for ourselves and to respect the spatial needs of others. During the pandemic, I watched how hosting virtual classes has altered my students' understandings of proprioception, and how it has altered the nature of classes themselves. The idea of how to cross the floor is challenging in a virtual classroom, both in regard to finding enough physical space to accomplish the exercise and in regard to the sense that all are watching. How can we reconfigure the act of being seen when it is mediated by a screen, when the dominant visual information in our spaces is not the people, but rather the various furnishings in our own rooms? How will that physical restriction affect our sense of proprioception? It remains to be seen as we continue living with different kinds of restrictions, whether they arise from public health concerns or simply from the changing living situations of older people.

Toward the end of the year in 2020, after months of working remotely, Dances for a Variable Population held a socially distant rehearsal. We chose to gather in an outdoor space in order to keep participants as safe as possible. Arriving in Washington Square Park, I recognized many people that I had not seen in person in a long while: Margaret, a shy woman who moved to New York from France; Joanne, a self-assured elementary school teacher; Raeann, a banker from Harlem; Hannah, a psychiatrist at Columbia Presbyterian. I saw Elsa for the very first time, as she was a dancer I had only ever met through online classes. I looked at each of them anew that day as we began to ready ourselves for class. I wondered silently to myself about what this time had meant to them, how it had affected their lives. Then, we began to move, and something astonishing happened. I watched as many of the dancers, even including shy Margaret, broke out in full and expressive movement—richer and more instinctual than before. Margaret had, in the past, been a reticent dancer: always very careful. A slight body, a wisp of a person, she surprised me often: she always volunteered to perform. She projected the aim to move in a large way, beyond her being, though I rarely saw her meet that aim before. That day in the park, however, she moved with rapture, lifting her arms and circling round and round. A delight to witness.

She was not alone with her dancing; we were all feeling those impulses. Joanne groped the ground, kneeling and coveting space joyously, moving as if suddenly freeing her demons. The collective improvisations developed, as Hannah ate up the space, swimming round and round. Normally a big mover, her movements grew and grew until they were more expansive than I have ever seen her dance. Even Raeann swayed her hips, getting larger and larger with each swing of the pendulum; and Elsa, shyly at first and then with confidence, boldly lifted her arms and arched sideways in beauty. It was as though I were watching a series of blooming flowers after an endless winter. Yes, we had been in quarantine, and yes, isolation had changed these older dancers. But rather than hiding or feeling belittled or intimidated by our time in small spaces, they were taking up even more space. Their delight in proprioception had increased, and the shyness that previously reined in some dancers was forgotten. After a long hibernation period, the need to move and move big was coursing through us. When asked to create a phrase of movement publicly, each dancer knew where to begin, diving into swirls, rocks, and reaches. At last, these older bodies had space to see and be seen, and I could appreciate their beauty as individuals. It was an extraordinary day in the new outside world, suddenly free to dance. The world expanded, and so did the dancers. Proprioception claimed large. Even with masks and social distancing in place, we moved big.

When performing a dance on a new stage or in a different space, one needs to rehearse the altered spacing. But dancers also naturally adjust, just as we did that day. A choreographer may need to fine-tune, but ultimately one can often rely on the dancer's sense of expansion. It is almost like reading a map, you can triangulate your correct location on stage by using your fellow dancers as markers in space. The distances may increase or decrease, but your spatial relationship to the other dancers does not change. That is the beauty of choreography and learning dance: learned proprioception, regardless of how one learns it, is about relationships in space. That day working in Washington Square Park was an exceptional lesson in rediscovering a sense of expansion after our stage had shrunk to the size of our computer screen, and in regaining an intuitive knowledge of how far to move as we adapted to the new environment.

In addition to thinking proprioceptively in our improvisations that day, we also spent significant and joyful time practicing lunges. The group was so happy to step and lunge, to deeply engage their bodies and eat up space with their forward motion. They progressed to lunging in all directions, freely alternating with various positions of arms and turns of heads—in order to see where they were going. There is a particular power in stepping lunges. When you step out into space, you take the chance of stepping into the unknown. You are literally propelling yourself forward into a new place.

It is easier to step side to side, harder to step forward and even harder to step back. Most older adults slip while stepping back—it is hard to precisely intuit space that is difficult to size up visually. The area behind you is important to see: you can turn your head to look behind, but then you also must have the fluidity of function in the neck to turn. Again, we encounter the connection between mind-body connection and proprioception: you must have a sense of what your body must do internally in order to accomplish an outward movement, and project that movement into space.

The idea of stepping in any direction is invaluable, however. In many ways, lunges are an excellent example of all the work we have engaged up to this point. Lifting one's feet is the key, just like in the exercises we learned through Matilda: lifting the legs is critical to avoiding stumbles. In order to accomplish this, in order to move with ease, we must build up our strength and engage with the lessons we learned from balance, namely, how to shift our weight while relating to our center.[2]

This shifting of weight is crucial to dancing and to mobility. With feet firmly planted in front, to the side, in back, the lunge moves you to a new place. You must proprioceptively navigate the awareness of where you are, and where you want to go with integrity. People are tentative about stepping backward—and rightly so, as you have to know where you are stepping to navigate safely.

Proprioception is also useful in understanding directions, the larger picture of where you are and where to head. Just as I had had proprioceptive problems dancing in *The Nutcracker* at the Pacific Northwest Ballet and getting lost in the choreography, I was also getting lost on a more spiritual level. I was losing my sense of self; my awareness of my own limits, where my body began and ended, what the right space for me to be in, was eroding, corroding, falling away.

Early in my time as an apprentice at Pacific Northwest Ballet, I was cast in a new production of *Swan Lake* directed by Kent Stowell, an alumnus of New York City Ballet. All I needed to do was stay well, take care of myself, stay uninjured. I was so thrilled to be in a company, to be noticed for my dancing; I was even mentioned in the review of the production. The review stated:

> One of the particular delights of watching *Swan Lake* is looking at the corps de ballet for signs of future Swan Queens. Naomi Goldberg is a Pacific Northwest Ballet apprentice whose first real appearance was as one of the Swan Maidens. Her small head with exquisite features, and her long, swan's neck mark her as a dancer to watch in the coming years as she perfects her technique.[3]

I was a dancer to watch. In the coming years, I imagined perfecting my technique and becoming the Swan Queen. A soloist, a principal dancer!

My future was laid out, my destiny mapped. But the truth is, I was way off-course. My proprioceptive skills as a dancer, knowing where I was spatially, knowing where to go on stage—they did translate to not knowing where I was going in my own life. I was not headed in a straight line toward being Swan Queen. My path was a spiral, pointing straight down. I was so far from the road pointing toward Swan Queen; I was on the road to destroy my future, my world, all that I loved.

I remember taking the bus to the ballet company for morning class in the Wallingford from the U District where I lived and stopping off to get an apple crisp, and then devouring and vomiting it up before class to relieve the stress I was feeling. No wonder I became slimmer and slimmer, it was the one part of my life I could attempt to control.

But I could not control my eating. I could not feel good about myself, I could not enjoy dancing, living with myself. I found solace in food, overeating and purging, then trying to remember the choreography and failing. Never mind my plan of staying well and healthy and strong: I ended up injured with repeated tendinitis, which led to shaky balance. I was so far from the game plan, miles from the balance I had been seeking.

Dancing at that time did not feel full or real to me. Now I realize how young I was, but then I thought I was grown. How much further would I go! Ironically, for our production of *Swan Lake*, Gelsey Kirkland came out to be our guest artist. I could not believe I would be dancing alongside my childhood hero—the dancer who, through watching her en pointe, taught me the miracle of balance. I could not wait to learn from her—and I did learn, though not the lesson I had anticipated. A dancer knows where they are through proprioception and their spatial relationship to others; through my spatial proximity to Gelsey Kirkland, I discovered something about who I was. During those performances of *Swan Lake*, I realized I could never gain greatness and freedom of expression in the world of ballet. Not the way Kirkland could. It was a highlight of my life to stand in the shadow next to her, and I knew that was a sign of my career as a ballet dancer. I had accomplished something, I knew that. But I knew, almost calmly, quietly, that I was in the wrong place. Call it spiritual proprioception.

Sam came into my life soon after that. I had a day off from the theater and decided to take myself out somewhere, take my mind and body away from the pressures of the ballet. I decided to go to a retro movie house that served popcorn all day. It was there I encountered Sam. He was a fire eater, a circus performer, from an exotic world very far from ballet. Not long after while performing Balanchine's *La Valse*, I injured my ankle and could not dance the rest of the season. I had to leave the ballet company after sustaining injuries to my ankle ligaments, caused by inadequate strengthening wearing pointe shoes. I needed the summer to take a rest from that kind of physical movement and physical strain. I hopped into Sam's light blue Volkswagen Beetle, and off we went on a Caravan tour of summer festivals through Canada and the West Coast.

It was through Sam that I was first introduced to the Flying Karamazov Brothers, a traveling troupe of performers, and a team of serious jugglers. They were new vaudevillians, and as such, they had a profound disregard for high aesthetics and the snobbery that came with certain kinds of cultural pursuits, like ballet. But there I was—a ballet dancer among a group of comedians and iconoclasts—and in a way, their disdain for ballet was a relief.

With the Karamazovs, we were out of the theater and, initially, I was out of my comfort zone. I was there, with my long hair pulled back into my typical ballet bun, but now I was wearing a tie-dyed t-shirt and improvising dances as the Rainbow Man sang songs and played guitar. It was a whole new world. There was no proscenium, no stage, no orchestra pit. There was no wall between me and the audience—that had been a wall I had needed in order not to be overwhelmed. But in this carnival-style work, something shifted. There was no gulf between the audience and the performers, and I no longer needed such space. The audience and I were in direct relationship to one another, sharing, crossing, and eliminating boundaries. There was an immediacy to our relationship. The traditional hierarchy of performer and audience was dissolved. We were all important; we made each other important. The immediacy of that shared participation was powerful, it awakened something inside of me that had been dormant for a long time.

I was transported back to a time, much earlier in my life, when movement was simply about joy. All I wanted to do was to share that joy with anyone and everyone around me. I remember being eleven years old, gathering my friends and classmates, and choreographing a dance for all to perform. Even then, I made space for each person to contribute their own solos. I do not know how I could have intuited this at the time, but I instinctively knew: everyone is a creator and therefore must be treated as such. To me, it was essential that everyone be the author of their own movement with their own bodies. I still, to this day, wish for all beings to present themselves and move for others in the way they feel best. We all know our bodies better than anyone else. The drive to be able to express this is the core of my teaching, and has been since I was a child, dancing in the lunchroom auditorium of my school. There we all were, in our leotards and dance shoes, performing pieces each of the dancers had created themselves. The finale was choreographed by me, of course. I was eleven, I was not so altruistic that I would give up the finale.

Much of my experience that summer with the Flying Karamazov Brothers brought me back to moments of my childhood, creating movement sequences without judgment, without limitation, with a freedom of imagination that let me explore my body and the shapes it could make through movement. As I invented movement in response to the Rainbow Man's music, I rediscovered the freedom improvisation could bring and the healing it could bring to my body and my creative soul. Like remembering the words to a favorite song from childhood, I remembered the thrill of dancing exactly the way I felt in my body. And I immediately could see improvisation's healing properties. The power of being understood, and the immediacy of shared expression, of creating something in real time, in tandem. Creating something that only I could make, and only with the people present in the room at the time. Rediscovering myself.

2

INTERMEZZO

Metamorphosis

Moving from One to Many

When you are truly connected to dance, a kind of alchemy takes place. There is a deep and profound awareness of your body—your own particulars, your own contours, the specific workings of your muscles as you move. And yet at the same time you become aware of a presence, a force outside of yourself that seems to be wordlessly guiding your movement. Although it is just you alone, you begin to connect to something larger. You are not only your body, you are beyond your body as well. I am reminded of a phrase from Shakespeare's *A Midsummer Night's Dream* describing the feeling of a magical, mysterious love. The character Helena, in awe of the human before her, calls him "mine own, and not mine own."[1] This too is the alchemy of dance. Our bodies are our own and not our own—as we move, we create a bridge between our physical selves, that working mass of muscle and tissue and bone, and our spiritual selves, our life-force, our collective dream, our larger humanity. In that space, we are both of ourselves and outside ourselves, both a single body and communing with something larger. We are in a flow state that seems to tie us, via invisible threads, to the traditions, people, bodies that came before. All this flows through us so that though we are singular, the act of dancing seems to multiply us outward. Through the act of dance, we are transformed.

Thus far, this book has focused on the dancer as a singular entity, the focus has been on a single body at a time. We will now, however, move into material that asks us to expand our gaze from the individual to larger groups, to forge connections, to create in tandem. We will move in communion with others, and through that communal action, alchemize new movements that one person could not accomplish alone. In subsequent chapters, I will invite you to perform different kinds of exercises that reflect this change in our thinking and our approach. I went on a similar journey from one to many as I metamorphosed from a soloist to the leader of a company. I transformed out of the traditions and routines I inherited as a ballerina toward a life that embraced collective creation, dance for all, and an entirely new normal for myself.

"I don't normally do this," I said, speaking into a microphone. "I'm a dancer, and um, dancers don't normally talk."

I squinted out into the darkness in front of me. I was on a small stage, with nothing but a microphone stand and a wooden stool. And when I say small, I mean small. Between me and those two objects, the stage was packed. This was not a stage for a corps de ballet or a group of modern dancers. It was a stage designed for a single performer: specifically, a stand-up comedian.

"So, as a dancer, normally I communicate with this," I said, indicating my body, "and not with this." I pointed at my mouth.

A couple of chuckles came from the crowd.

"But, um, it's a comedy club. So I guess I have to talk a bit."

I was performing my regular set at the LA Laugh Factory comedy club. I was not a traditional comedienne by any stretch. But no matter: I would be there, at the comedy club, every single night. It was me and the open-mic regulars, the whole group of us trying to get an opportunity to perform, no matter what. Normally, the open-mic crowd had to wait to go on until the end of the night, after the more established, programmed comedians had performed. But I would tell whoever was holding the clipboard that I had to wake up early for dance classes and could not wait until 2:00 a.m. to perform. I told the guy in charge to put me on as "the dance break." And that did it: I was on.

I would usually start my routine with some version of the Dancers Don't Normally Talk bit, and then I would stop talking and start dancing. I would invite the club audience to join me onstage and dance something, anything. They could follow me or make up something new—I played a cassette I found, *The Classical Hits of the Seventeenth Century*, and they were free to just move to the music. Magical things came out of that freedom. I loved the moments when I saw someone surprise themselves. The people at the comedy clubs were certainly surprised by me. But it was a stage, and a stage was all I needed. If I wanted to dance, to experiment, to try new things with my art form, I needed a space and an audience. I learned not to be picky about the space. An opportunity to dance was an opportunity to dance, and that was what I was able to find in Los Angeles more than anywhere else.

In LA, I was not going to fit dance into my life. I was not going to squeeze in a lunchtime session here or there. I also, however, was not going to squeeze myself into the narrow idea of existence that a life in professional ballet was offering. Los Angeles did not even have a professional ballet company at the time. Regardless, I was determined: I would not adhere to any prescribed model of how to live. I was going to choreograph my own life, and dance was going to be a central part of it.

This self-making was possible in a city like Los Angeles. Los Angeles was a place that was open to new ideas; a place where it felt possible to start anything. For me, Los Angeles was the city of the individual, while New York was the city of the collective. At that time, I found in LA the freedom to experiment and become just who I was, nothing less, nothing more. While in New York, one may have needed a long legacy, a glowing resume of dance experience, and webs of impressive connections in order to dance professionally. In LA, I could find part-time work easily and dance literally anywhere.

When I landed in the city, I lived with one of my oldest friends, Susan, and her family. Susan and I were very close from our days dancing in the School of American Ballet. She had recently lost her job dancing with the Cleveland Ballet and was living back home in the Valley. Her family welcomed me into their home, I think to help Susan recover from the difficulty of that loss. Losing that job, and that ballet way of life, catapulted Susan into a deep depression. The draw of a life spent training in dance is hard to replace. The daily practice of 10:00 a.m. class, the constant assessment of how one's body feels throughout the day, the rhythm of rehearsing by day and performing at night can be almost like an addiction. Every second is poured into how loose your muscles are, monitoring if anything hurts which might hinder your practice. And you are rewarded with the constant high of being on stage. You are not just rewriting your schedule when you leave the professional ballet world—you are rewriting the moment-to-moment relationship with your body, the part of ourselves we can never separate from.

I understood Susan: leaving the professional ballet life behind had been hard for me, too. I knew how it felt to miss the structure of that world, its simple but rigorous daily routine. But I had gone to another world after leaving the professional ballet model: I had gone to college, I had danced with the Flying Karamazov Brothers. I had encountered other ways to meet the world, and these experiences left me convinced that all people could feel that full sense of the body, not only ballet dancers steeped in the culture all day. I wanted to introduce Susan to this more open way of thinking about dance and movement—I wanted to introduce everyone to that idea. But as of yet, I did not know how to transform that philosophy into a practice.

In the meantime, I found work. In LA, I could work part-time and continue dancing. I danced in ballet classes with Stephan Wenta, a Polish ballet teacher who taught popular evening classes. I danced in performances on small stages, like the newly constructed performance space by Tim Miller called Highways in Santa Monica, in downtown LA at the LACE in performances with my newfound idol John Fleck, and at the comedy club. During the rest of my time, I hunted for opportunities to make money and have health insurance. In this, I learned an early lesson, and an invaluable one: it is possible to welcome dance into one's life without abandoning one's responsibilities. One does not need to throw away daily routines, the security of life, in order to dance. You don't need to be a professional dancer to make space for movement in your life. Our world unfortunately often encourages this sense of imbalance, telling us that if you are a professional artist, you sacrifice stability, and if you have chosen a stable career, you do not have the time or right to be creative. I caution against that rigid thinking; life doesn't have to be all or nothing.

Think about the words "supporting yourself." We often use those words in reference to employment. We can apply that same idea to movement—embracing the dancer's connection with your body is also supporting yourself. Just as you commit to your career in order to "support yourself," you have to commit to a certain responsibility to supporting your body as well. It is like a work-life balance, only here it is a work-dance balance.

It was this balance between a life of dance and a responsible life that I sought in Los Angeles. The first thing I did was join the Screen Extras Guild. The only qualifications for work there were to have a "look," and I qualified in spades. I apparently had the "New York Look," which in Hollywood means all-black outfits, and I also had the "Young Mother Look." That was a surprise to me, as it would be years before I had a child of my own. But Hollywood was not pushy about reality, so I was not complaining. Between 1985 and 1986, I was an extra in dozens of movies and TV shows. Working as a film extra was the ideal job: I had secure employment and bizarre hours that fit my dance schedule. It was perfect.

Through creative thinking, hard work, and more than a little luck, I had put together a good life for myself—I could take ballet class whenever I wanted, exercise in the gym at the YMCA, and work enough in Hollywood to make it all make sense. I was carving space out for myself, taking the small, necessary steps to change my life. Within this framework, and with renewed dedication, I could incorporate the lessons of ballet, incorporate the lessons of regular strength training, and build something new. In addition to using the gym at the Hollywood Y, I also began to teach regular classes and rehearse new dances with my old friend Susan and a new friend Jeanine Ward. Jeanine and I met in David Nillo's class at the Hollywood Y. She was a classic California girl: slender and blonde with an amazing smile. It was not a surprise that she also worked as an extra in the movies. She was a loose mover, and that translated to her personality—she was incredibly fun to be around and a great improviser. It turned out she was teaching her own fitness class, and that gave me the idea and the confidence to start teaching as well. Though Hollywood can seem superficial, the bonds Jeanine, Susan, and I forged were very real. We believed in each other and supported each other. With Susan and Jeanine in my corner, I knew could make my own world of dancing. We were souls seeking a cause and community. We were making bold moves, and looking to make our own mark in the Tinseltown world that was Los Angeles.

Inspired by working with Susan and Jeanine, I found a new, unusual place to dance. This time, however, rather than going postage-stamp small with my stage, I was going to go big. Boardwalk big. Ocean big. Together, we turned Venice Beach into our next venue.

Between the comedy clubs, our work at the YMCA, and the many people I was encountering in the LA dance scene, I was honing not just new movements but new ideas about movement. I aimed to expand and practice those ideas at the beach. Just as there was no person more suited to dance, so too was there no place more appropriate for dance. Dance was for everyone and therefore for everywhere—you just needed to unlock the potential within each person and place. That summer, I set up shop in a covered area under one of the outdoor pagodas at Venice Beach as my studio. Just like at the comedy club, there was a "first come, first serve" culture at the beach when it came to reserving a spot. But we were relentless. We always snagged that third pagoda, our preferred location as it was central to Venice Beach, before the other performers on the board-walk had a chance. We could not be stopped! We were on a mission. That pagoda was my dance-theory laboratory, and Susan and I were devoted experimenters.

From there, I gave mini-performances and mini-classes directly on Venice Beach Boardwalk—open to all, with the goal of inspiring the masses to embrace movement in their lives, every day, wherever they might be. Susan and I decided to combine the idea of performance and education into one event rather than delineating sharply between the two. Our work on Venice Beach had elements of professional performance, audience participation, and group fitness classes. I chose group exercises that would inspire a somatic connection in people; I taught movements that would stretch common areas of tight muscles, could be activated in public spaces, and would bring about an understanding of opposing forces inside the body as part of the larger universe. I constantly asked myself what would inspire the people to move, and even more, what would in-spire them to move with understanding.

I would begin with a dance set, a duet or a solo, continuing into an im-provisation with audience participation. Then we would round out the set with prescribed exercises to improve flexibility and mobility. This model generally worked. Once we had a crowd gathered, we had to be brief, en-ergetic, efficient. We had to command their attention and be quick about it—we wanted to get to the meat of the show, the audience participation and the teaching of the exercises, and not lose the crowd during our per-formances. We decided each set would last about fifteen minutes and then we would take a break to sit, chat, and drink water.

Our favorite musical choices were "Eleanor Rigby" and "Imagine" by the Beatles, the Bach Preludes, and "Under the Boardwalk" by The Drift-ers. We would then throw in three minutes of a genuinely rocking tune from my trusty old cassette tape *The Classical Hits of the Seventeenth Cen-tury* and invite people from the crowd to dance with us. If that cassette worked at the comedy club, I had a good feeling it would work here too!

We led exercises like the Back Rack, which taught folks how to distrib-ute their body weight and share weight with one another. Cresting over the back of a friend, the student would lean onto a friend's back support-ing themselves by grounding their hips and legs. Susan and I had to teach how to support weight as well as give it—a new idea to many in order to successfully share weight, rather than unsafely falling all over your partner like a sack of potatoes. This exercise required us to describe the idea of center and how to share it: what it means to take the weight of another body using your core and lower body, and not forcibly pull them onto over your back with your arms; how to make the motion a smooth transition, how to open your shoulders and ribcage. It was a challenge, but a rewarding one, for two trained ballerinas to try and put into new words the ideas of center that had become so second nature to us. We also taught something called the Pull, with the goal of really feeling a rounded spine. Similarly, it was a teaching task to guide the audience into making the back round, to evenly pull away with their bellybuttons toward the back of the body to create a stretch on the back: a variation of a contraction from modern dance. For those familiar with dance, the shape is intuitive. But for others, creating an even, satisfying curve of the spine in order to open one's back was challenging and required precise explanations. Susan and I were learning to break down our knowledge, step by step.

For our last exercise, the goal was to find the loose motion of a swing. One has to drop through to the heel, allowing the foot to brush the floor and loosening the muscles of the legs and hips, achieving a dropping sensation of the working leg. This can be difficult to master as well, but the lessons are invaluable.[2] Local beachgoers eagerly gathered to see us dance and to practice the exercises themselves. We made the event official: our act was called The Ballet Girls, advertised with two paper signs posted on trash cans that announced our show, "Beatles! Bach! Beach! And Exercises for All!" We became very organized in our set: we were presenting a quirky series of three short duets and solos set to the music we had access to for the first part of our set, and then encouraging audience participation by leading three exercises for the crowd.

We were ballet girls gone rogue. We danced in sneakers and dresses, shorts, all sorts of layers of clothing. A sense of freedom and joy permeated everything; we were profoundly happy to be outside at Venice Beach, just dancing and moving however we pleased and not wearing pointe shoes. My mother was appalled. When she came to visit and saw me on the boardwalk, she wailed, "From the stages of the grandest opera houses to a beach! My daughter! I am going home!" And she did. But we could not cling to tradition, we were dancing what we believed, living up to our principles, sounding the alarm for free expression. Free movement for all! Dance without bounds! California gave us the space to be outside, the nice weather to gather crowds, and that brand of Los Angeles attitude that encouraged an individual to step out of the crowd and make a name for herself.

My litany of experiences was growing, and so was my community at Venice Beach. Regular fans would gather each weekend to applaud and participate, from young kids to older adults. I remember one man in particular; he was in his early seventies and rode a multicolored, well-used bicycle. Instead of throwing dollar bills into the hat we left out for donations, he would throw in thick socks. Every weekend, he would have new, fresh pairs of socks for Susan and me. He told us, smiling, "Dancers always need socks." And he was correct, we did need socks. We became dependent on this regular sock donation and eagerly anticipated seeing him ride up once a week. One day, when he came by with his sock delivery, he found me smoking a cigarette. He never came back after that, he was so disappointed in me. I realized the heightened position I held—I had become a symbol of health in his eyes, and I had let him down. I quit smoking shortly after that experience, and I insist that all teachers at DVP set examples of good health. There on Venice Beach, however, I had not yet realized that by involving the audience, my performance was teaching. I was already a teacher; I just needed more tools.

Around this time I recognized that I also needed a more stable job. Working as an extra was great when I was getting started and needed maximal flexibility, but as my routine began to solidify around me, my needs began to change. I needed work I could rely on, with specific hours, so I could be sure of the time I needed for exercise as well as training and performances. Once again, my new friends showed me an unexpected way forward. Jeanine had recently received her credentials to become a substitute teacher, and she suggested I do the same. I received an emergency credential as a substitute teacher in the elementary schools of LA.

In a way, substitute teaching was not unlike learning a new role in a performance: it was like being an understudy for the full-time teacher. There were new steps to learn, and a new style, but I felt this kind of performance was a process with which I was familiar. I could think of the students not as students but as an audience. Even though I was often filling in for a teacher that had left behind no script, I could improvise. All that meant was learning the language of my new audience: how to hold their attention, how to tell a story of authority with my voice and body, how to impart a narrative to them that would take root in their imaginations and minds. These were adjustments I could make; I had learned how to change through my life on the stage.

Eventually, I noticed a pattern. It went like this. Day One: I had a great day planned! I arrived with bells on. It felt like I had creative projects coming out of my ears. Day Two: I had a pretty good plan for the day. The students seemed happy enough that I came back, and any projects we did not finish the previous day, we tackled. Day Three: Could I come up with something? Day Four: no more plans. Gone. Fresh out of plans.

I learned two things from this pattern. First: only take jobs that are three days or fewer. Second: I would need to stretch myself beyond the role of performer in front of these students. Just as I realized more about my status as a role model to the man with the socks, I quickly discovered that in school I needed to be the director, not the actor; the choreographer, not the dancer. I needed to improvise and have a plan. I was being looked to as a leader, and I needed to learn how to embody that role elegantly. The qualities of leadership that I had to possess, however—time management, discipline, incentivizing, curriculum building—those I had to seriously develop, and quickly I ended up substitute teaching for ten years in Los Angeles, first with the elementary school system and later in the middle and high schools.

This period of my life reminds me of a story about the Duomo in Florence, the magnificent dome of the cathedral of Santa Maria del Fiore built during the fifteenth century. The foundational stone had been laid in 1296 under the guidance of architect Arnolfo di Cambio, who died soon after construction began. While construction slowed, by 1366 the nave had been built, and it was time to build the dome. However, the technology did not exist to safely build a dome of the proportions suggested in the design. The leaders of the city had faith that given the spirit of the age, someone would invent the technology in time to complete the structure. And they were right. The city announced a design competition, and different models for completing the cathedral were submitted. A model submitted by goldsmith and clockmaker Filippo Brunelleschi appeared promising. In March 1446, the first stone of the dome was consecrated by the cardinal of Florence, and this awe-inspiring building stands to this day.[3] But I am struck by the metaphor inside of that story. One must have the materials, the building blocks to start, to create a foundation, as well as the kiss of boldness, the flare of imagination, the wildness of dream to complete the full idea.

As I was teaching, I was inadvertently acquiring the skills I needed to run a company and fulfill my larger dream of a dance company for everyone. I was observing the flaws of our educational system. There was little time set aside for using the body, and little to no time spent educating and building a somatic understanding in young people. When teaching for a full day, I knew I needed time for my body, and I was positive the children needed that time as well; learning to feel one's muscles, to tie together, to unfold, to loosen, to connect our parts. By forcing children to remain sedentary most days, we are subconsciously teaching them to neglect their bodies. By not addressing the need for physical movement, we are asking students to pretend that their bodies do not exist, that they are not important to attend to. But the body requires attention as well. School systems have to set aside time for the body, just as we in our daily practice must choose to set aside time for our bodies.

One part of my future Duomo was my work as a substitute teacher, acquiring leadership and managerial experience, witnessing the ways in which our society encourages a static existence, and trying to unite large groups of sometimes unruly individuals. Imagine those lessons as a series of wooden beams. Set them aside. We will use those to build something magnificent.

Meanwhile, my experiences at the comedy clubs, at the Hollywood YMCA, on Venice Beach, with schoolchildren, were all beginning to coalesce, although I could not define it just yet. But these moments, these essential lessons of dance that I was picking up in mysterious places like breadcrumbs, or like more and more piles of wooden beams, were pointing me in a new direction. And that direction was collaboration. Enter three choreographer-dancers into my life—Larry Hyman, Daniel Albert, and Roxanne Steinberg. Together, collaboratively, we formed Dance Diner.

On the surface, we were not an intuitive match, the four of us. We could not have been more different in terms of our dance backgrounds. Daniel Albert danced with Bella Lewitsky's company—he was trained in serious modern dance technique, as well as jazz, and did a lot of commercial work in the film world. Roxanne Steinberg also had modern dance training, but a different specialization. After studying in Japan with the artist Min Tanaka, she fell in love with Butoh, a Japanese form of modern dance developed by Hijikata Tatsumi and Ohno Kazuo in the 1960s. Butoh was

Dance Diner at the basketball court in the Hollywood YMCA. In photo:
(*L to R*) Roxanne Steinberg, Yehuda (Larry) Hyman, Naomi Goldberg Haas,
and Danny Albert, 1988.

originally named *ankoku butō*, which meant dance of darkness,[4] but it
also became known as the dance form which "resists fixity."[5] Roxanne embraced both the gravity of this movement and its ambition to continue
to push the boundaries of what constitutes contemporary dance theater.
Larry Hyman, now Yehuda Hyman, was the most experienced choreographer among us, and it was his vision that gathered us all together. As
different as we were in our training, we were united in our ethics, in the
principles behind our dancing. Using the time I set aside from my teach-

ing, we began to work and experiment together. We used the YMCA gym for our rehearsals—the very same gym where David Nillo held class. As we delved into our work creating new choreography, each of our different styles and influences clashed and collided. It was as though we were working on one canvas, and we each had our own distinct color of paint. Over the period of one year we choreographed collaboratively and individually, maintaining our own aesthetic but staying united by the common effort to make dance accessible to all audiences: both those who were dance savvy and those who were nothing but sets of left feet.

Dance Diner performed in a monthly series of concerts and group events. We had begun in the same gymnasium that David Nillo had used for class, but once we began our monthly events, we shifted to using the basketball court. It was essential for our purposes that our performances take place in an untraditional performance space. We had been trained for formal dance halls, but our artistic mission insisted upon a space with no preconceptions or signifiers of superiority. We were right to set our work there: we filled that gym with 100 to 200 people every single event. Each performance followed a certain structure. The opening numbers would always be followed by a cheer written, spoken, and danced by all four of us. We would then perform a series of dances for the audience, mixing formally choreographed compositions with improvisations. The core of the group was the four of us, but we would often have guests in the show, and we would always have an audience participation number. That was my contribution to the particular mission of Dance Diner. Each of us had his or her own focus, his or her own hypothesis about dance that we were working through, and incorporating the audience was mine. I knew it aligned with my belief that everyone can dance, not just the folks given the title of "dancer," but I was not entirely sure how best to pull it off.

One afternoon, I talked with Larry.

"OK, I know the idea of teaching the audience dance steps feels right to me. But . . ."

"But what?" Larry asked.

"But what if they just won't do it? What if it turns into one of those awful audience participation shows where no one participates?"

"Well . . ."

"And then it's just awful! We'll just be standing there, mute, staring at them, completely hanging out to dry on stage—"

"Basketball court," Larry interjected.

"You know what I mean! How do we invite them to join? How can we welcome them into the movement, and not force them into the movement?"

We mulled it over. And suddenly, Larry said, "Maybe we're making this more complicated than we have to."

"What do you mean?"

"I think the fastest way to get people on your side is just: feed them."

A true eureka moment. So simple, so effective. Laughing, we were delighted by the idea of drawing the playful parallel between nourishing one's body through art and movement and nourishing one's body through food. One is just as essential as the other, when you think about it! Feed your body what it craves, food and movement!

We fed the audience candy, we fed them pizza. I am sure we were not the only people to get pizzas delivered to the Y, but we may have been the only people who got pizza delivered for a crowd of 200. In some ways, it was a cheap trick. We wanted them to like us, but it worked. As the audience munched on treats, they warmed up to us. When we asked them to join in and learn a few movements, they were receptive. My experiment was underway.

Each month, each performance, I investigated the different ways an audience could be involved. We tried teaching the audience a simple sequence in real time. We tried asking them to imitate various movements they'd already seen in performance or a rehearsal. To me, it did not matter so much what they did, as the action of doing it.

We were always trying to push the boundaries of our work. Our aim was to surprise and to subvert. One of our basketball court performances in 1988 began in almost total darkness. The only light came from the gym's weight room on the second level of the gymnasium. It was a windowed space, protected by chain-link fencing, and the weak light from inside that space shone thinly through the window, falling on the basketball court below. In the near darkness, the only noise was the high, tense, nerve-tingling sound of violin strings, like a classic horror film. One by one, the fluorescent lights of the weight room flickered to life. Then slowly the three ceiling fans turned on, seemingly autonomously, animating the space with a quotidian movement turned strange in the unsettling atmosphere. Other noises began to emerge as the fans moved faster and faster:

more textures in the music itself, but also sounds that were harder to identify. The sound of hands on metal. The sound of rattling chains. Slowly,
the source of the noise became clear: four dancers (the four of us) were
climbing the chain-link fence. Up, up, high above the audience. Our bodies were silhouetted a deep black in the harsh light pouring through the
second-level windows. The shapes we made with our bodies were grue-
some, animal-like, as though we were haunted or possessed. The music
crescendoed, the strings playing higher and higher and louder and louder
and faster and faster, until a moment of silence, when one of us shouted,
in a voice like a vampire "Dance Diner!" Then we all dramatically shrieked
like B-Movie starlets from a 1940s horror film. Oh, I can't tell you how
fun it was! But fun was part of the point. We saw dance as something essential, not frilly or artificial or formal, and we sought to strip off its clas-
sist associations and overly serious attitude. We saw dance as food for the
community—a vital necessity everyone was entitled to.

The first time I took both my choreography and my method of teaching
dancers seriously was with the creation of *Looking in a Fishtank*. While I
developed the choreography for this dance in my time with Dance Diner, I
remember thinking of how to create the dance during a moment when my
mind was completely free of stress, allowed to wander, and could connect
disparate ideas together in mind, impulsively, almost without thinking. I
was in a space where the raw materials were present, and I was not forcing
them into any shape. It felt like they assembled and built something on
their own.

I had this time because I had been in a horrible car accident and gotten
a prescription session with a massage therapist. After substitute teaching
one afternoon, a drunk driver in a truck had run over my Toyota at a stop
light. My lightweight car had crumpled, and the only undamaged space
was the seat I had been sitting in. I had to stay overnight in the hospital
because the doctors wanted to be sure I did not have any internal injuries.
But I had been very lucky, both in regards to the accident, and because
I had the health insurance to give me access to those massage sessions.
Sometimes I still long for those times on the massage table, where my
mind could float, and I could imagine dances. Time like that is invaluable
for the artist—for anyone, really. I was learning again to trust that once
the building blocks are present, it only takes space, vision, and belief for
them to begin to form something magical. Time for relaxation is a part of

Looking in a Fishtank. In photo: (*L to R*) Debra Nelson Schonfeld, Naomi Goldberg Haas, and Hope Urban. © Blake Little Photography, 2024.

that recipe, time to relish and be grateful for our bodies and minds. Rest is essential for the seeds of dreams to germinate.

The piece I had been ruminating on during my massage sessions was titled *Looking in a Fishtank*. It grew out of small seeds of thought into a full performance featuring a group of twenty-five dancers, an exceptional ensemble to choreograph for. The piece was created and performed in the Dance Kaleidoscope festival at Cal State LA by a medley of trained and untrained dancers of all ages. It was a partially choreographed dance, set to J. S. Bach's English Suites. Rather than giving the performers complete carte blanche to move however they pleased, I had typed out a score, or physical script, outlining the very specific movements they were to perform. The improvised element came in the choice of which movement the untrained dancer might choose.

We held three different rehearsals, all of which took place in the community room at the Hollywood YMCA. Dancers came from everywhere: from my classes, from Dance Diner, from my performing life around

Venice Beach and the comedy clubs, from strangers I had only recently met. Each person involved in the piece received the typewritten score and practiced it with whoever was in the room that day. I had no idea how many people received the score, or how many would be dancing in the performance. Much was left to chance, especially in the mostly improvised Pavane section. We knew the Pavane section would be bookended by trained dancers with set choreography, and that for the finale there would be trained dancers of diverse shapes and sizes performing their own improvised movements with their own score, but we could not predict at all what the Pavane section would look like. Anything could happen. It was a leap of faith.[6]

In addition to the semi-improvised sections, *Looking in a Fishtank* had components that allowed me to flex my choreographic muscles in a more cohesive way. The piece contained solos, trios, quartets of dancers, all dancing in a way that asked a question or explored a particular concept of movement or performance. Johnny, a compact guy with black curly hair and a powerful jump, danced a solo that came played with ideas of discovery and disappearance. He would appear on stage, then disappear in the wings, then burst forth again. On and off, on and off. Two ballet dancers, Susan and Debra, a trained dancer who had recently torn her ACL and was in recovery wearing a knee brace while performing, danced a minuet and a trio with me, structured from the idea of following each other, dancing quick and fast steps.

My favorite section of *Looking in a Fishtank* was a quartet. Four dancers crossed the stage in one line, horizontally from stage left to right. They were all facing front, essentially attached to one another and never breaking some kind of physical contact. These dancers moved with the same step pattern, a zigzag step, like a grapevine but in tight sync with the dancers next to them. All the while, they kept a perfectly straight line. It perhaps sounds simple, but it was incredibly difficult to pull off. I had trained dancers perform this section, as it was difficult to maintain the pattern of the legs while moving their attached arms across each other, and of course, never looking down at their feet.

My suspicions, my hunches about movement, had been true all along: the delight of the unknown can be captivating. It is unexpected and endearing, like a dog or baby onstage, a being who responds with pure impulse, who has no inhibitions or insecurities affecting their behavior. Or it is entirely present, like a trained dancer, perhaps, but in the midst of a discovery, a movement he or she cannot predict. I felt sure that untrained dancers, armed with the strength of connecting to their own bodies and prepared with a physical vocabulary of steps, could perform. After the premier of *Looking in a Fishtank*, I came to the conclusion that while improvisation and the use of a score could be a tool to use in rehearsal in order to develop dances, it was too risky in live performance. But what I did get right was this: the rigidity of the structure of the overall piece created an immense sense of freedom in the dancing of it. The dancers embraced light heartedness and fun and a complete lack of inhibition. The power of these adults, performing with the innocence of babies and the magnetism of animals onstage, encouraged us to organize a company where this spirit of movement could happen, and could happen for more and more people.

My philosophy of dance for everyone that I had been developing, experimenting with on the Venice Beach Boardwalk and exploring with the audiences at Dance Diner, was not just a philosophy anymore. Movement for all was not simply a theory in my brain. It was a real practice, formally encountering the world.

I arrived in LA in the mid-80s with a suspicion, a hunch about the work I wanted to make and the philosophy I wanted to live by. I believed that dance was for everybody and every body. I believed that dance transcended ideas about class, race, tradition, access. This hunch was strong, but at the same time fragile. I believed in my ideas, but when I arrived, I did not have the tools to realize them. But by the end of the decade my job as a teacher had given me tools to lead with rigor, experience in organization and plan-making, and connections to all different kinds of communities. My work with Dance Diner gave me an outlet for expressing my true aesthetic and my true artistic self, an opportunity to continue my experiments in audience participation, a team of collaborators, and a stab at seeing what life in a company would be.

Setting the Foundation

Los Angeles Modern Dance and Ballet

Looking in a Fishtank performed for one night only, and it was our debut performance as the Los Angeles Modern Dance & Ballet (LAMD&B). It was this dance that earned us the title "The People's Ballet," a title I wore like a badge of honor. The Company incorporated as a nonprofit in 1989 and operated in Los Angeles until 1998. From 1998 to 2003, we continued adding and mixing in dancers from New York City, and took our work everywhere, performing in Florida, Texas, Los Angeles, and New York. Our most active period was from 1994 to 1998, when we had a regular coordinated program with LA-based communities and produced a mix of large-scale productions performed by, with, and for the community, with a calendar of annual shows performed by a troupe of trained dancers.

Throughout Los Angeles are distinct communities of people living, working, playing, dancing together from San Pedro to East LA, from Leimert Park, South Central, and Santa Monica to Los Feliz, Silverlake, and Pasadena. With the Los Angeles Modern Dance & Ballet we taught these distinct groups and created specific dances, each with their own aesthetic and style reflecting the people within those communities. School children in San Pedro, young mothers and toddlers in South Central, families of grandparents and young people in East LA, older adults in Pasadena, young families in Los Feliz and Silverlake, and athletes in Santa Monica—each group had distinct cultures, histories, and interests. We built on these distinctions through dance-making, ultimately culminating with a performance for and with the community we were engaging with.

For the Poinsettia Park project in West Hollywood, we garnered family support in teaching dance to children in the large local community center. Situated inside a massive space for dancing and armed with a crop of after-school children, we set a physical score, much like the idea behind the Pavane section of *Looking in a Fishtank*. This score functioned almost like a menu, letting the children know what kind of movements were available

Naomi Goldberg Haas, *KlezDanz*, Ford Amphitheater, Los Angeles. Photo © Craig Schwartz Photography.

to them and encouraging them to choose which movements they wanted to perform, how, and when. Maybe on the score there was the option to leap across the floor—one child might leap across the floor quickly, repeatedly, over and over. Another child may look at that same item on the score and choose to leap once, right at the very end. This score allowed for an incredible amount of both freedom and structure. A beautiful paradox.

We had set up a set of portable stage flats on either side of the stage, and the children were to cross, using creative movement, from one side to the other. They would use the area hidden behind the flat as a backstage, a place to wait and listen for their cues in the music. Instead of playing the Bach suites that we used in *Looking in a Fishtank*, however, we danced to the orchestral music of John Adams. It was a bold choice artistically and technically: John Adams's music proved very difficult to count. With dance, choreography is often based on a count of eight. Imagine choreographers in movies saying, ". . . and a 5, 6, 7, 8!" This count allows the dancers to follow where they are in the music and to match their movements to the rhythm. With this John Adams piece, however, the downbeat (or the first count in the set) was difficult to hear. If we wanted the children to enter confidently to perform their cross, then they needed to be sure of when their entrances and exits were within the music. It was imperative that every child discover their own way of turning and running across the stage and for them to feel ownership of their moment in the music. Therefore, we made an adjustment. Rather than use an aurally complicated piece of unfamiliar music, we came up with something new, creating dances with set choreography performed by trained company dancers and included all or our new non-dance trained participants who presented their own personal variations of the movement that we originally generated. This way everyone had their own movement-moment to shine from within the group. Thus the *Grande Finale* was born.

The *Grande Finale* was to be a new dance, set to the eminently recognizable *Blue Danube Waltz* by Johann Strauss II. It was planned for audiences of all ages: not only people involved in the rehearsal process, but those sitting in the bleachers who were inspired to learn our dance with us and hop up on stage. After the penultimate number of our performance, we would inform the audience that they would learn, and could be a part of, the *Grande Finale*, if they so chose. Hands would shoot into the air. The members of the audience would then congregate "backstage," behind the flats on stage right or stage left. Then, following a dancer or teacher from our group, they would appear on stage, making a diagonal or horizontal cross and performing the lead dancer's movements. Kicks, leaps . . . the movements were big and space-eating. The *Grande Finale* began as a means to incorporate large groups of people into the performance, all dancing a set step in the best way they could. The idea proved to be inspired. We built audiences and ensembles from all over Southern California, dancing in gyms with our makeshift flats. The idea was so successful that it inspired an official "Spring Gym tour" in 1993, which reached audiences all the way from the Mojave Desert to Irvine.

We performed multiple versions of the *Grande Finale* in many different locations, but it was at the very first one, in Poinsettia Park, that I witnessed how infectious dancing could be. Seeing groups of people dance together created surprises that went beyond choreography. There was a tenor of truth in witnessing that moment, for all involved. We come to the theater to see truth, to see people reacting to each other in real time, but often we are looking at artifice. In these performances, we are, of course, watching the result of rehearsal. Nothing is discovered, everything is planned. There are some performers who make us forget that we are watching something scripted, through their talent and artistry, but these artists are few and far between. Most of the time, we are watching people who are well-trained and well-rehearsed, but perhaps have lost the thing that made them original and strange. The spark of liveness is not there. Most of the time, we are looking at the ideas of a director or a choreographer, rather than the ideas of the people embodying action on stage. But here, with this performance in Poinsettia Park, we started cracking open the idea of what is pretend, what is pre-planned, and what is real. What happened in that moment, with that performance, will never happen again. And you could feel that energy in the crowd—the feeling of witnessing something special, something once in a lifetime. The Poinsettia Park show was when I saw that moment of glory, of mastery, of composition, of surprise.[1]

Perhaps you are wondering at the balletic nature of these movements, and the balletic vocabulary. Chasse. Battement. How did words like these, and moves like these, interact with different communities? Maybe the answer will surprise you, as it did me during this phase in my life. I myself had often felt alienated by the formality of ballet. The terms are literally in a different language! I could imagine students from all different communities feeling left out of that world. The opposite happened, however. Perhaps because of the circumstances we built in the room, with the students and their ability to both learn and choose their movements, the verbal and physical language of ballet felt accessible to them.

We took the *Grande Finale* concept and transformed it into various school projects for the Los Angeles Modern Dance & Ballet.

The company hired Nick Gunn, an ex–Paul Taylor dancer, and our company dancers Alissa Mello, Susan Castang, and Karen Acosta as teaching artists and held dance programs of Interactive performance and onsite workshops for the Los Angeles Music Center Education Division, the largest arts programming organization in the country, at the Los Angeles Music Center. The company created shows anywhere—myself and my fellow teaching artists would sometimes travel three hours outside of Central LA to work with communities that were often underserved by other arts organizations. Those projects brought me into contact with students from all over the LA area, and working with this diverse group of young people eventually led me to a series of discoveries about the universality of dance, movement, and self-expression with the body.

The professional dancers from the company performed a forty-five-minute show comprised of modern dance and ballet, interspliced with informal talk-backs, explaining the physical forms of ballet and the corresponding French terms for audiences of school children. At the end of the show was the *Grande Finale*, in which we took members of our young audience and taught them steps to do to be part of the finale. The rest of the audience also had a combination to learn and perform, giving all participants and audience members a chance to dance.

Working with the Music Center's Arts Education Division offering performances and dance workshops in elementary schools sometime two hours outside of downtown LA, I eagerly welcomed young people into the world of dance.

"Feel the porte de bras," I said, as I led exercises with an elementary school class from Leimert Park. They stared up at me as I raised my arms to model the movement. Then one by one, they tried it.

"Feel the lightness of your arms as they move through the air!"

I watched a look of both joy and calm appear on their young faces. I had anticipated resistance to ballet, but any resistance was melting away as the children began to move.

"Now point your toes!"

They did.

"Can you feel the different shapes in your body? The long lines? The circles?"

They nodded, smiling.

Later, we went to the Mojave Desert. This is a completely different demographic than Leimert Park, and yet the response to ballet was equally enthusiastic. There, the kids felt the rhythm of the waltz and loved the feeling of kicking their legs up high. Everywhere we went, the students were pulled, almost magnetically, into the movement of ballet. Its allure was strong throughout all of Los Angeles, including rural areas. I was shocked how young people from all different cultures, backgrounds, socioeconomic statuses all craved those movements. My personal journey had been so rooted in interrogating ballet, rebelling against the ideal form, and instead opening my mind to other dance traditions. Watching these young people gravitate toward ballet, however, I discovered how the physical actions could be appreciated no matter what body type you had. It represented the notion of working hard to really achieve something: the physical strength and knowledge to understand the sensation of a straight leg, to extend your leg behind while reaching the arms and lifting the front body, to kick your leg to the front while holding your back straight, the feeling of turning in a pirouette on one leg while lifting the other. I also see now that for us to go into these schools and welcome students into these movements was a powerful statement about accessibility. Our presence propagated the idea that ballet, often misrepresented as the most difficult of forms, was achievable and possible for everyone.

One of these projects, the San Pedro Dance Project, was a tiered mentoring program. We brought dance classes to five elementary schools and mentored local high school students, who in turn taught the younger school children. It was fun to work with the high school students—they were eager to learn and eager for the opportunity to dance with professionals. They passed this enthusiasm onto the younger students: they performed for the elementary school and then taught the young people themselves, transferring their love for dance to the generation one step behind them. It was a moving expression of community and lineage. Eventually the younger students would matriculate to high school, where they would then teach dance to the elementary school students.

That was what felt important here—the development of community through dance. Even though the students responded to ballet, they did not need correctly pointed feet to achieve the particular energy harnessed in the attempt to attain finesse. These students taught me to see ballet practice in a new light and to study the form to find alignment of the body without judgment, but rather with an emphasis of balance and strength. The kids I taught at San Pedro High School were more themselves in the versions of ballet technique we were discovering together—they were able to find themselves, their community, their version of physical health.

San Pedro Dance Project's work with communities in the Leimert Park area of South Central, Los Angeles, West Hollywood's Poinsettia Park, and our base in Los Feliz also directly shaped my later work with Movement Speaks. The Silverlake Jewish Community Center in Los Feliz held our studio and office. Students chipped in to install a new Marley floor, and donated mirrors to make an unused second-floor exercise room into a dance studio. The JCC was happy the space would be utilized and excited for a young dance company to refurbish and hold classes after school.

Our most successful classes were for the parents and older students wanting to move purposely and freely without judgment. We offered classes like beginning ballet and multimethod modern dance. Multimethod modern dance class pulled from many different movement influences: the study of yoga combined with the floor work of Martha Graham (specifically her contractions and their usefulness in getting down and up off the floor), with the tilts and balances of Cunningham, and the swings of José Limón technique. I learned these techniques from the Barnard College dance program, and I believed parts of each could be imparted to students. All these different types of movement were useful to teach, I thought, so rather than silo them into focused courses, I put all these ideas and influences into one class. It was a typical class time of one hour and a half, promising better health and the body of a dancer by practicing these methods. I wanted anyone and everyone to feel they could afford to dance, so we charged a low rate for classes. The important thing was the presence of the community itself.

I did care, however, about having a space of our own. I was proud of having an office, and I loved having use of a dance studio where we could teach and create dances at any time during the week or weekend. A lot of creation happened at the Silverlake JCC: from classes, to rehearsals, to performances, to costume crafting in the parking lot on Sundays after our run throughs, to making flip books with quotes from current, LA-based playwrights with our board of directors. With that space as a home base, it felt like anything was possible.

This era of my life was an incredibly productive time. I did work with the Mark Taper Forum Theater choreographing dances for the MainStage productions. As a resident choreographer at the Mark Taper, I was able to make dances with playwright Eduardo Machado (*Floating Island*) directed by Oskar Eustis. I created choreography for Joanna, a beauty who uses a wheelchair, creating a Tango set to Piazzolla music.

Joanna continued to dance with LAMD&B in our production of the *Twelve Dancing Princesses*, which premiered at the John Anson Ford Amphitheater with a company of twelve women and girls, ranging in ages from six to eighty. This dance was my first formal attempt at making choreography with older adults and younger dancers together. I was thrilled at the possibility and elicited help from all the different corners of my life to bring the piece to light. LAMD&B board member and Mark Taper Forum Associate Director, Corey Madden, wrote the script. Donna DiNovelli, a New York playwright and librettist, wrote additional poetry for the project. Hilda, a performer I knew from my days in David Nillo's class, danced in the piece. We had the honor of having John Fleck as our narrator, an artist who had gained infamy for being one of the NEA Four whose funding grants were denied due to obscenity on stage. We had big names, certainly, but the piece was also built by small acts of devotion: one Sunday, after rehearsal, all the dancers met in the empty JCC parking lot and spent the afternoon sewing flowers and twigs into the tulle of their tutus. It was a strange and beautiful contrast, for a strange and beautiful group. We performed Twelve Princesses annually at the John Anson Ford Amphitheater, an outdoor venue in the Hollywood Hills.

I was teaching the multimethod modern dance class at JCC Silverlake when I first noticed—my hands. They looked different to me. I gazed down at them. I stretched my fingers wide. I balled them into a fist. In this shape especially it was clear, my fingers and knuckles were getting exceptionally swollen. In an instant, my mind flashed to images of Martha Graham's hands—her hand movements were very particular and essential to her particular style, so they stood out. She had the same swelling in her hands. I thought to myself, "Must be all this Martha Graham floor work that I'm doing in class. I'm channeling her!" The thing is: Martha Graham's hands came from an ailment. She had arthritis. I, however, was neither channeling Martha nor developing arthritis. Something else was in store for me, but I could not look it in the face yet. I kept on with the belief that the swelling was a result of teaching Graham for a while, until the truth insisted upon itself. In fact, it stopped me in my tracks.

First, I got dizzy during an LA Modern Dance & Ballet performance at Poinsettia Park, almost falling down while dancing a spin. Then, I had a fever that would not come down. I went home to New Jersey shortly thereafter to see my parents, although it was not to be a normal visit. Suddenly, while at home, I found I could not move my arms because I was so stiff and swollen. I went up to bed to try to give myself the restorative power of sleep. But for days, all I could do was remain in bed. For the first time in my life, I did not dance. More than that, I did not move. It was one of the only times ever that I did not move my body. Lying in that bed, neglecting motion, every illness and every pain suddenly jumped out of wherever it had been hiding in my body, and I could not ignore them or will them to go away. My parents convinced me to get medical attention. When I returned to LA, I took their advice and went to the doctor. It was then I learned what was happening to me. It was then I was diagnosed with lupus.

Lupus, or systemic lupus erythematosus, occurs when the body's immune system attacks its own tissues. Symptoms like inflammation, fever, and fatigue occur periodically, often interspersed with periods of remission.[2] I believe that dancing masked, as well as relieved, many of my symptoms. Through wonderful doctors, I was given treatments that allowed me to keep dancing. But I carry that diagnosis with me. There is no escaping it, there is only simply moving through it.

LA has changed so much since it was my home. It is strange to know it is the same city where I spent my formative years. I have changed so much because LA was my home—in easy and difficult ways. I began my life there with a few scattered notions about dance and about myself. I had so many questions, and I thought that made me unstable. I had a wobbly foundation beneath my feet. I wondered: How could I best teach dance? How could I best live dance? What were the necessary ingredients to creating choreography that was both compelling artistically and compelling spiritually, holistically? Could those be the same thing? Where was my place? Who were my people?

KlezDanz at Luckman Theater, Los Angeles, 1985. In photo: Nicholas Gunn and Naomi Goldberg Haas. Photo by Rose Eichenbaum.

Those destabilizing questions led me to discoveries which strengthened me, rather than shook me. They started me on quests for the necessary materials with which to build my life. Running around the city—from comedy clubs to Venice Beach, from the Hollywood YMCA to a Silverlake lot—I was accumulating knowledge about the various spaces dance can fill: the places dance feels like home in, and the places that dance does belong even if everyone tells you that it does not. I learned about the intricacies of audience participation through experimenting on different scales—one person at a time in the comedy club, small groups clustering around us on the Venice Beach Boardwalk, large audiences at Dance Diner, all the way to *Grande Finales* in schools across the district. I learned how to be a teacher: how to model behavior, how to assemble a curriculum, how to lead with authority, how to work in a team. I learned the strength of having a plan; the power of repetition, expectation, praise, and consistency; the grounding that comes from timeliness and goal-setting;

and the happiness of surprise, flexibility, shifting a plan. In LA, I met the collaborators that would shape me into the dancer and choreographer I am today. I began my first company. I learned, deep in my bones, the importance of community work and communal dance for people all around the city. I had children jumping up out of their seats to participate in group movement, a testament to the power and deep necessity of physical education in schools. I began to learn in a new way the power of regular movement—through moving, I could manage my lupus. I worked odd jobs, I worked good jobs. I worked hard, and for that, LA granted me the tools. I was ready to build.

But for me, LA was not a place for building. LA is largely flat, horizontal. No, if I wanted to build—to build up and up and up, to finish my Duomo, the architectural feat of my life—I needed to build skyscrapers. So I went where the skyscrapers are and flew back to New York.

3

ALL TOGETHER NOW

Roundup, Duffy Square, Times Square. In photo: Maxine Steinhaus, Rocky Bostick, and others in Times Square, 2012. Photo © Ka-Man Tse.

Growing Upward

New York

In LA I learned who I was, the individual pieces I am made of. New York City would be the place where I gathered people around me, like a solar system, to build something through our movements in tandem. While in LA I got to know the unique rhythms of different schools, families, groups; in New York, my mission was to bring all disparate groups together.

The return to New York was an incremental process. It began as a way to spend some time with Brian Kulick, my soon-to-be husband. We had met when he was an assistant director at the Mark Taper Forum theatre in Los Angeles, then he went off to be a resident director at The Public Theater in New York. We had a long-distance relationship as I continued to run LA Modern Dance & Ballet out of California. For several years, I flew back and forth: to New York, and to California for rehearsals and performances with my company. Eventually, I knew I had to make a choice, not only for me, but for my family. Brian and I had our son, Noah, in 1999. As a baby and a toddler, he was with me constantly, happily crawling around rehearsal studio floors, keeping himself entertained with his own curiosities. I could rehearse in the studio and trust that he would be safe, due to a combination of his limited mobility and the watchful eyes of my friends and fellow dancers. When we performed, Noah would be a part of it, dancing in the school shows and joining in on *Grande Finales*. He would wander onto the stage, often with a toy car as a companion, and participate in the movement along with everyone else. But as he grew older and was involved with other productions, I knew my time taking him to LA with me was ending. As a baby, he was happy playing with a bottle and crawling all over the studio, but after he conquered walking, he was his own force in the rehearsal room.

It was clear that I needed to make an adjustment if I were to continue being dedicated to teaching and creating choreography and being the kind of mother I wanted to be. I also needed to think about the kind of daughter I wanted to be: at that time, my mother had been diagnosed with the chronic cell leukemia that would eventually kill her. I committed to New York full-time. It was a permanent home for our family and the end of my life and work in Los Angeles.

I was back in New York with a loving husband, a perennially happy baby boy, and a newfound and much healthier relationship with my mother. I spent my days taking my mother to various doctors, looking after my son, and attending NYU Tisch School of the Arts to get a master's degree in dance. It was in this strange state of being simultaneously overwhelmed but not fully engaged that I walked into Coles Gym at NYU. From the outside it was a rather nondescript cream-colored, air-raid-looking-bunker, but inside it was my idea of paradise. There was the familiar screech of sneakers against the gleaming maple floors of the basketball court; the sight of people with their hair and t-shirts unapologetically drenched in perspiration; the feel of cool air-conditioning that could not quite quell the collective heat of all those bodies working out; and the intoxicating scent of sweat, chlorine from the pool, and just a hint of disinfectant. I felt an immediate rush of joy run throughout my entire body. I thought to myself: I can make something out of this.

This time I would not be dancing in the gymnasium space, like I had been in LA. Instead, I was teaching strength training. Fifteen years after initially learning weight training and muscle strengthening for my own health while working an office job in San Francisco, I was applying that same knowledge and teaching strength-building to older adults, many of whom were struggling with health issues. As opposed to substitute teaching, which had felt like a combination between a crash course and a crash landing on an alien planet, teaching the strength training was a bit like coming home after a long time away. I was familiar with the gym environment, familiar with the machines themselves, familiar with the necessary steps to accumulate muscle. And now I was teaching adults, and older adults at that. Many of the core tenets of teaching that I had acquired through substituting were still applicable with the group of older adults, but fundamentally, adults choose to be in class. Teaching adults who opted into class every day was a different atmosphere. There was no need for any incentives; the adults were paying attention, and I did not need to monitor their focus in the same way I had with children. Now that I had their attention, I had to ask myself: What do I do with it? Their choice to be there made for a different dynamic and prompted different questions about progress, process, planning, and retention. How do I encourage them to keep coming back? What will hook them into class? How can I personalize the work to both deepen somatic understanding and also create an atmosphere that people want to be in?

I thought about my students, my new audience. I drew upon the physical knowledge I had acquired, as well as the knowledge that I had picked up working with different communities in LA and tailoring movement to different bodies. I began developing methods specifically for older adults to gain strength and gain a deeper understanding of the major muscle groups impacted by age. I studied senior fitness, and practiced my techniques with my longtime colleague, Eleanor. We were an excellent team. Eleanor had taught this strength-building class for years before, but she was not a dancer. I looked at her practices through my own lens and saw the ways that dance could be incorporated into the atmosphere of the weight room. I glimpsed how lessons of dance, if not dance itself, could inform these older students' understanding of their muscles. I began addressing the students as though they were dancers, asking them to think about their physical alignment and their movement with mindfulness. The older students from the West Village who enrolled in that class inspired me greatly. From this strength-building class, I built dance classes for seniors. And from those dance classes, I built a company.

Dances for a Variable Population was officially formed in 2005 out of my Dance and Strength Training Classes, many of these students became core company members. Out of this new phase of work came our Movement Speaks program. Movement Speaks codified those initial classes and became a system of shared movements and exercises drawn from a variety of dance forms (classical, modern, folk, and contemporary), fitness, and most importantly ways to activate to personal expression. We believe that such an exploration engenders greater physical and mental health while promoting social connection and improved quality of life for all. We began with choreography for older adults in performance at the Public Theatre in a play by Suzan-Lori Parks, as well as in other offshoot venues like Bushwick warehouse spaces in Brooklyn, the theater in Merce Cunningham's loft studio in Westbeth in the West Village of Manhattan, and the Henry Street Settlement on the Lower East Side. We incorporated in 2009 with our formal production of *Fanfare* at the Terminal for the Staten Island Ferry, which was produced by the River to River Festival and the Lower Manhattan Cultural Council.

I completed my degree from NYU and, through Dances for a Variable Population, graduated into a community. My life and company in New York are defined by the ways in which we come together—artistically and physically through dance, and also socially. I write those terms as though they are distinct from each other; however, the artistic, the physical, and the social are all linked through dance. Dancing is social in its very being. In its most essential, even stripped of the conscious idea of dance, movement is an act of communication. You wave to a person—that is a physical gesture that communicates "hello." You cross your arms, and perhaps you are communicating reticence, or impatience. The body is constantly in social contact through its physical expression. Even if you were to remain still, you can sense being watched, and can sense how your own movements are making another person feel.

Physical impressions are powerful, both in our conscious and unconscious minds. If you close your eyes, for example, you might be able to summon the movements of an important person in your life. I remember the posture of my grandmother, the way she stood or sat in a particular place. The memory is clearer than remembering her face. The expression of the face is often more fluid; the memory of physical presence is clearer. I say all this to align ourselves to the idea that movement is not a solitary act, but designed to unite, to bring us together. Movement Speaks, in its celebration of dance and older dancers specifically, is therefore a celebration of togetherness and the social health and happiness of older people.

New York City's population of older adults face significant physical, mental, and emotional risk factors and issues. These issues could be high rates of obesity, diabetes, hypertension, depression, low rates of more-than-moderate exercise, and social isolation. These challenges are even more extreme among low-income senior populations, who have higher rates of obesity, hypertension, and diabetes. Even before the COVID-19 pandemic, loneliness was at epidemic levels, affecting 60 percent–80 percent of the population, decreasing life span by 26 percent.[1] COVID has only increased this isolation.

It is well-studied and well-documented that social interactions are vital to happiness and living well, and this is even more true for the older adults. Gathering people together to dance in tandem is an essential social comfort.

Imagine that you are in a Movement Speaks class. Look around the room. Who might you see? Who might you want to get to know? Lottie, with a husband who has Alzheimer's disease, finds the dance class especially rewarding for the possibilities of movements she finds, attending class daily and consistently making new choices, often silly ones. She dances with pain in her knees yet knows class will make her feel better. The strength of social ties is visible even in the smallest moments; it can be as minor as seeing the same people in class every week, so that if one person is not there, everyone notices and wonders where they are. The sense of community is a matter of being looked out for, on the large and small scale. You continue to look around the room. Do you see Colette? Oh, there she is. Colette is a sensitive partner, always aware of her proprioceptive personal space. She was once a performing dancer, walking on stilts and turning with ease. She now suffers from Parkinson's, diagnosed a few years ago, and she uses dance to keep moving with ease, but is forever aware of her increasing problems. Small and fragile, Colette always moves lyrically, even when confronted with the challenges of Parkinson's. There is Lucy, a ferocious partner, flying through the space without any sense of hesitation. A woman with uncontrolled glee, she will try anything and everything, a consummate partner if one has the courage to dance with her. Formidable and strong, with a presence to commit to any action, from rolling on the floor to spinning on her feet. She is the first person to enter the room when we are preparing for a class and the last to leave. Her presence is known and loved. Social comfort through dance is finding a new friend who is also looking for companionship: someone to invent a movement with, someone to show your cool new move, someone to co-create and choreograph with. And there is Jackie, the artist. A sculptor who moves the way her art looks, Jackie loves angularity, straight lines, sharp corners. She is unwaveringly herself and knows what thrills her artistically. You may want to get to know her more.

Finding Our First Steps

Once in LA, I went to a lunch with David Nillo and two of his students after we had all been dancing in his class at the Hollywood Y. It was a delight to savor the satisfaction of both really moving, and of joining others for a meal after that exertion. It was wonderful that such a group would go out together, and I remember thinking to myself, "This—this sense of community—it will happen for you. Later in your life, you too can create this." And it has happened—through dance, I have made incredible friends and connections during class and in the moments of relaxation and satisfaction that follow.

I have seen the ways powerful new moments take shape when people encounter new partners, new wellsprings of ideas and experiences. When you share a task with someone, and with a time limit, you immediately connect on a new level because both of you have to agree on something, and agree fast. For example, let us say your task is to create a canon, a series of repeated movements with a partner over the course of ten minutes. You do not have time to be worried about social anxiety or loneliness: you have a project to do, and limited time to do it. And while there is a distinct end to achieving the task, I have witnessed the lifelong friendships that arise from a quick, five-minute assignment.

One of my favorite moments in class has become (paradoxically) the end of class. Obviously less dancing happens in this period of time, but I nonetheless get to witness something magical being created. I watch the conversations that began through dance continue, as the older adults leave the room and go off to have a meal or a coffee together after class and catch up on their lives. It transports me back years earlier, to lunch with David and his two students. Dancing together inspires community, inside the practice room and beyond.

Often one witnesses another's dancing and is inspired by their moves. This is social connection; someone understanding another nonverbally. A new move is created that was not there before, and a conversation is born. This social interaction naturally became another source for choreography and expressive movement. Intrigued by the ways in which we physicalize social connection, I developed an exercise for our Movement Speaks class. In this exercise, movement really does speak, as a student physically enacts a gesture of greeting. The first dancer enacts a greeting in movement. The partner responds, holding their "answer" for a moment. The original mover then responds with another new movement, creating a conversation. As this exercise progresses, people grow increasingly comfortable with each other socially, at the same time as they grow more comfortable with creative movement. This movement conversation is often people's first attempt at glorious, improvised dance.[1]

Now you have acquired the building blocks, the individual skills, the choice to make dance a priority. As you read along, you are beginning to experiment with expressive movement. You may be intimidated by the idea of dancing. How do I come up with movements? What if I have no ideas? First, there are no bad movements. All movement is good. Second, you do not need to reinvent the wheel every time you choose to dance. Think about the Movement Conversation exercise again. You are essentially having a regular conversation, just like you normally would. The only difference is now you are looking at that conversation through the lens of dance. Looking at all movement through the lens of dance leads you to the life of a dancer.

To begin thinking as a dancer and living as a dancer, we just have to alter our vision a bit. We are already moving all the time, even in very small ways. It just takes a little spark, just a small touch of boldness, to transform that daily movement into dance. Improvisation is an essential tool for unlocking creative movement and alchemizing quotidian movement into something expressive, poetic, and creative. Improvisation is a gateway to individual expression. Once you have developed the necessary tools to begin safely and confidently moving—the somatic understanding of the mind-body connection, muscle strength, physical mobility, proprioception—how does your body like to move? What physical sensations do you gravitate toward? How can you begin to dance, express, emote, create? How can we unleash our potential as movers and dancers and leave unhealthy judgments behind? For indeed, there are so many ways our minds like to shut our imaginations down, before we even start.

Let us pretend, for example, that you are in a dance studio, standing tall and still, ready to dance but unsure where to begin. You breathe. You are awaiting instruction. Your body is strong and ready to move. Yet when the instruction comes, it is this: make a tree. "OK," you think. "Make a tree. Got it." You pause, "But . . . actually . . . what does that mean?" You have an image of a tree in your mind. But the tree looks nothing like you, really, so . . . how do you make a tree as you dance? "Am I doing this correctly?" you ask yourself. "This feels wrong."

I would argue that this prompt sets you up to fail. A prompt like "Make a tree" emphasizes stasis as opposed to movement. It is asking you to embody something large, full, and complete unto itself. That is too much to do! I find that breaking down the body into particular elements can be helpful in improvising. Instead think about how you, in your body, would embrace the movement of a tree. How do you imagine and embody the sway of a tree's branches? Or the grounded sense of the tree's roots, shooting deep and strong into the earth? Can you relate your spinal column getting longer, growing upward toward the crown of your head, to the trunk of the tree? These questions invite you to be inside a moment of movement, rather than a static idea, object, or state. Instead of thinking that your whole self should become or imitate the entirety of a tree, let yourself explore one body part at a time. Dip a toe into a movement. Start incredibly small and become comfortable within a minute gesture. This comfort will beckon you toward greater physical boldness and adventures with improvisation. Just begin. Movement begets movement. You may be surprised at the way the tiniest micro gesture can grow.

You can even begin improvising here, as you read, from where you sit. You only need to move one hand. Raise it out in front of you. Take note of its shape. Begin playing with the fingers—can you spread them wide? Wiggle them? Try opening and closing your hand. Take some time now. Explore just these movements and sensations for a moment. Play with different combinations of movement. When we narrow our focus, it is amazing how many movements spring to mind. You do not need to invent anything—just cast your attention onto even the smallest area of your own body, and movement will guide you to imagination.[2]

With every student, every dancer, I offer this: find what inspires you. Find what enchants, delights, captures your imagination. Find what feels good in your body. Only move from a comfortable place. Explore from a place of freedom, as well as ever-increasing understanding of what feels good in the body. Some ways of moving may be uncomfortable—that's OK! Try at your level. For example, maybe you can swing your arms, but while swinging your legs, you hold onto something to maintain balance. This way you get the experience and sensation in your body while acknowledging the needs of the body. Maybe you can circle your hips, but not your head; your wrists, but not your knees. All of that is OK. There are no wrong interpretations of movement.

Everyone must feel safe in the dance space: that is an important key in order to improvise and create. As a leader of the class, or even as a solo dancer trying to exercise in his or her living room, one has to develop an atmosphere that immediately lets everyone in the room know that there are no wrong choices. From the beginning of a Movement Speaks class, we ask students to try out movement patterns. These patterns could be as simple as extending the arms and pulling them in—back and forth. We use a rhythmic pattern and ask students to demonstrate so they can assume leadership of their chosen movement. The simpler the movement, the better. It should be something everyone can do and repeat.

We call this exercise Passing, and we begin by standing in a circle, where everyone can see each other. One person at a time is the leader and all must follow her movements. We ask for a rhythmic lead, something that repeats: an arm moving up and down, in and out, or a leg kicking is a good example. These are movements that in general, everyone can follow. We generally do this exercise at the beginning of class, in a format that alternates the movement between being teacher-led and student-led. Alternating back and forth between teacher and student is a key way to create a safe or brave space: students do not feel pressure to generate ideas, and their choices are encouraged. The exercise promotes the idea that there are no wrong choices. All movements are viable, and the first choice is usually the best choice—so just go with that! The only requirement is to find the beat and move along with it. Moving along with the music necessitates making choices quickly, but often that little bit of pressure frees your mind from your own judgment. You learn to move with your own instincts when you do not give your brain too much time to judge or doubt.

We move around the circle so everyone is prepared for their turn to lead. When we moved our lessons to a remote format in the time of CO-VID, we used Zoom tools to spotlight people when it was their turn to lead. This ended up being surprising at times. Suddenly all eyes are on you, waiting for you to make a move. It can be tricky to know what to do in the moment, but that is part of the idea of the exercise. One must take responsibility for the integration of one's own movement and make choices.

Some students are more naturally leaders, while some do not identify with the role right away. But by alternating between student and teacher, we create a net of safety, in which you can take one action that gets you closer to moving with confidence. For just one movement, you can be a leader. In class, in life, in your body. It is a boost of energy when you create something, no matter how small, and know that whatever you chose was exactly right for you. Because again, all movement is good. The movement you make today in class is more than what you walked in with—that is an achievement to be acknowledged with gratitude. Every body is made for dancing—it is simply a matter of discovering how to find support, safety, and brave expression in dance.

In a way, improv is all about short-circuiting the inhibitions we have around dance, around feeling silly, around the pressure we put on ourselves to be "perfect," around making the wrong choice. We have learned how to approach large ideas, and we have started fast to prevent second-guessing ourselves. Now I will introduce you to another tool of improv: action words. Action words are full of movement, rather than representational nouns which are static. Action words are the heart of exploring. It is much easier to perform an action than it is to be an object. It might be difficult to think about how to be popcorn, for example. Popcorn is still, and crunchy, and rests one piece on top of the other in a bowl. That is not the easiest state for a human to emulate. But can you pop? Yes! You know what it is to pop up, to jump, to do what popcorn does when it moves. What are other action words you can think of? Can you strike? Glide? Bounce? Slice? Move in angles? Move in curves? Can you feel the difference between one action and another? Popping parts of the body feels very different than dancing in a smooth, continuous dynamic.

Sensing moments of suspension in your body—swinging side to side, forward and back—is different than shaping an arm into a round space and finding a place to hold that shape. By playing with opposites, my older adult students in NYC could feel the difference in the manner of the movement in our own bodies, rather than being told there was a difference. I developed an exercise to share the possibilities of different ways of moving with different body parts at different levels in space. A guided, free movement experience, the Dynamics exercise directs continuous movement in varying ways. This exercise presents an opportunity to move in different ways, explore what is possible for each of our individual bodies, and experience new sensations and expressions through movement. It is key to explore each dynamic in different body parts, at different levels, at different speeds. Commit to one action and move with it—throughout your entire body. Again, you can start small if that's what you need. But let the action grow.

"What floats?" the teacher asks the whole class. She has asked the students to float, but first asks for common thoughts about what that action word might mean, physically. She repeats the answers out loud as they come in. "Boats float, yes. Snow! Great. Dust floats through the air in a really different way, yes!" She supports the individual imagination in movement. "Now let's begin to sense floating with our bodies. Imagine leaves. Snow. Dandelion seeds on the wind." The students in the class begin to move.

"Work with the multidirectionality of floating in your arms . . . your legs . . . maybe a smaller body part, your hand? Your head? Your heart?" The nature of the explorations change—they grow more specific, more creative, more attuned to their own particular bodies. "Do we have a sense of what all these different kinds of 'floating' might have in common? Maybe it's that the action has no focus." She asks the class to float at different levels. "High! Middle! Low!" At different distances now—"Close, now far!" And then from different relationships with another person, making different shapes of the body, in circles, wide, small, using different body parts, maybe just one arm, hand or the full body in action.

Then the teacher changes to a contrasting action. "OK, everyone. Strike! This action uses focus and moves toward one direction. Strike out your body parts: an arm! A leg! An elbow! OK, now strike your total body in a lunge. Use different levels and different parts of the body. Strike high, strike low with both arms, strike to the side."

The class changes its energy as the movement dynamic changes. The teacher and students move onto "bounce" as a dynamic. The teacher finds the action by describing it. Jiggle, move loosely like Jello, or like a rubber band, like anything that reverberates. Create an action that has a rebound sense. Commit to a bounce of an arm, full body, a leg. "As you move ask yourself: What is possible and easy to bounce? Maybe your head, maybe your two legs?" The class moves from a bounce back to a float, then a striking action, back to a bounce and freeze together.

Dynamics is interesting because of its melding of the individual and the group. As you are exploring, the group starts to make decisions together. Everyone explores one dynamic, and then slowly shifts, through listening and observing, to a different dynamic. Everyone is making their own decisions about how the dynamic works on their body, so they are all technically moving differently, but the dynamic functions like a uniting theme. A compelling dance emerges from the chaos of improvisation.

In class, we typically play jazz music during this exercise in order to highlight the different ways of moving. The terminology we use for the Dynamics exercise derives from the Dance Education Laboratory at the 92nd Street Y (DEL): I learned this way to teach dynamics, using words like "glide" and "pop" and "float" and the teaching of simple choreographic tools from Jody Arnhold, director and founder and inspiring leader of DEL at the 92nd Street Y, and her associate Ann Biddle, who in turn were originally inspired by Rudolf Laban and his tools for movement improvisation.

It is particularly powerful to stand amid a group of people and move in one, unified dynamic. The group can "feel" when to make changes. This is a physical skill that is developed when working as an ensemble. Dancers can sense change. Unison is developed among a group of dancers. It is always interesting to see the group consensus. When one person changes actions, we all follow along, an example of saying "yes" to the group.

This sense of the group is not innate, however. That sense must be developed, and not everyone embraces it immediately. From the beginning of taking classes, Ingrid, a sturdy, 5' 2", Berlin-born New Yorker, made enormous changes. Often bringing her German friends to dance class, she boasted about what she was learning. Dance was her vehicle for expression and health, and exercise became her new way of life after retirement. She frequently said that dancing was keeping her alive and that her transformation could be attributed to the fact that she was dancing.

During our annual performance in Washington Square Park, Ingrid blossomed. As we rehearsed for the performance in the studio, we discovered how important it was to find a way for Ingrid to relate to choreography, to be able to repeat combinations but also not feel restricted. How could we allow her natural innate movement to be visible, but connected to the other dancers? We created two dances with her, both requiring improvisation with landmarks embedded. When gathered in one area, all dancers could find places to raise their arms or move low. How they moved from one landmark to the other was the individual dancer's choice. One of the two dances was built from movement that workers in the field made to make wine. Initially, I thought Ingrid would take to the wine makers, imagining her response to creating wine. She quickly loved performing the picking of the grapes in an imaginary vineyard and stomping her feet in a vat of grapes. When it came time to close the dance, however, she had difficulty following unison in the group, as the music required counts without clear markers for changes. But Ingrid's energy was infectious. She loved to stomp grapes—a moment highly physical and felt throughout the room!

The second dance was a group choreography that required all dancers to relate to one another in a sequence set prior to rehearsal but new to this group based on strong musical cues for changes. Ingrid loved the music and the feeling of being part of a larger composition. While she often poorly remembered the structure, she was a standout when performing the many individual movements. She particularly loved whenever we "reached," performing a reach to the sky as if meaning poured out of her, reaching to the heavens like we should all be reaching upward. The dance had these opportunities for her to soar!

Watching Ingrid, I learned how important it was to embrace the individual qualities that make one human in performance and in class. Dancing helps people remember who they are when they bare themselves. We know who we are by our relationship to the group. Dance is about the melding of the individual and the group: it is an act of communion. A gesture of togetherness.

Communion, community, and improvisation are related. When we encounter new people from new places, when we mingle and mix, we are building new spaces in our brains, learning new words in our emotional vocabulary. There have been studies done which show that a key to maintaining plasticity in the brain is the discovery of alternate ways to perform a task. When I first heard this theory, it was explained to me in geographical terms: if you take the same route home every day, your brain will stop creating new cells, new memories. The key to building the brain is to find a new way home. Improvisation is not pulling ideas out of the air, it is looking around you, or looking at a map, and simply finding a new way home. Find a new way home in the movements you try, in the different people you meet outside of your community.

In Movement Speaks, we often literally asked our students to find a new way home when we took them to perform in public spaces all around the city. When busing the older adults to perform in public parks in new neighborhoods, we used to say, "We just want to expand your world!" Busing older adults to West Harlem from Queens to perform at Grant's Tomb expanded their sense of what they were capable of just as significantly as the dance they performed. On another occasion, we put together a culmination event, wherein seniors from the West Village took the train uptown to meet older adults from Harlem in a community center gym for a performance and a celebration. Each group had separately practiced the same exercises, and now everyone was going to perform together with the same purpose. That gathering was a magnificent collision of experiences and expanded everyone's world. An important part of the effort of Movement Speaks is to bring people together—both to fight the epidemic of social isolation and to find artistic inspiration.

The new ideas collide with our inherited ideas and create something new, similar to the play of opposites that we have been exercising through the mind-body connection. The body works in opposite—as your leg stretches back behind you, you engage the front of your body. As you reach out to new people, experience new neighborhoods, you are able to renew your relationship with your past, your culture, yourself. It is all forward and backward, give and take, lead and follow. That is a lesson of dance. Dancing is about passing energy back and forth to create something new: energy between you and the audience, between you and your dance partner, between you and the group, between an individual and their community. Each component contributes something to the overarching story—a movement, a shape, a color, a spirit. In passing ideas back and forth with movement as our common language, we often create something entirely collaborative, something that could not have existed with ourselves alone. We specifically explore these kinds of juxtapositions with dances and improvisations in partnerships.

The concept of working together to make a dance is new to many people. Working together is an opportunity for problem-solving, innovation, and inspiration. The teachers set up a problem before the group, and then everyone needs to participate in order to solve it. We ask for some movement, and more often than not, there are people who take charge and make decisions for the rest. We celebrate people embracing new roles and ownership over the movement that inspires them. We also want to encourage those who are hesitant about leading to have that opportunity as well.

A wonderful experience is dancing with one another in a partnered format and changing leadership by following directly behind another. When one person is done, she simply turns around and her partner becomes the leader. Let us watch different couples perform this changing leadership exercise. Lucy, a large personality with plenty of ideas of movements, was leading Molly, always worried about whether or not she was dancing correctly. Lucy was a big and confident mover with striking blonde hair—she always moved very fully. She was not afraid to try new things, and she was never worried about being wrong. Quite the opposite of Molly, who was terrified of making mistakes. Molly first connected with me when I was teaching fitness classes at NYU, and she stayed with me when I transitioned to dance. She loved the fitness element, but she was reluctant to dance. There was something about the creativity dance required that she did not love, but the clarity of fitness suited her—she was not required to make decisions, she just had to follow instructions in a fitness class. She was a perfect person to work with Lucy, sampling Lucy's way of movement when she was the follower. The act of trying these new moves changed how Molly imagined dances. Lucy's bravado and large movements altered the direction of Molly's dancing ideas.

In another part of the room, Colette was leading and following Talia. They were a more similar pairing, but their similarities did not stop them from challenging and encouraging each other to experiment with new movements. They both were attached to the world of ballet. Colette was an accomplished dancer who danced professionally when she was younger. Her recent Parkinson's diagnosis complicated her ease as a mover, but she still loved to improvise when she felt comfortable with her balance. Her movement patterns tended toward the balletic and acrobatic, even as she worked within the constraints of her diagnosis. Talia was also a former dancer, though she never danced professionally. Her years of ballet lessons when she was younger continue to exert sway over her dancing vocabulary, and the training she received in her younger days lent her a lot of confidence in class. Just like Colette, Talia also experienced some limitations in her movement because of back pain, but she is not daunted. They were also a perfect pairing, in a way different from Lucy and Molly. Colette felt confident experimenting with new ideas from her past dancing days, knowing Talia would follow and present new challenges when she took over as leader. Both women rejoiced in testing dance phrases that satisfied them.

Lottie was also inspired by the exercise of following a partner. She had been a student of mine for over twelve years—she started in my class at the NYU gym but had never taken a dance class. When she joined us in Movement Speaks, she took the prompt of following one person as an opportunity to experience creative movement. Before she officially joined dance classes, I knew Lottie was interested in dance, as she shyly admitted previously loving Zumba classes when she had previously lived in Florida. Even though she had only participated in fitness classes with me, her strong personality and heart, matched with her vigorous movement, indicated that she would make a good candidate for classes in dance. When she joined the class and we asked her to follow another dancer, the task stretched her imagination and inspired her to pull ideas from Zumba and everything else she could think of. Lottie has gone on the create dances built from her huge personality and has deeply embraced the values of dancing.

Julie experimented with this exercise as an opportunity to discover her own movements and new ones. She found working with just one other person enough of a challenge; she does not have to dance with a group. Often she likes the chance to mirror her partner. Facing each other, one partner performs a movement while the other partner imitates them, creating the effect of a mirror. Julie likes to both mirror and follow; she chooses partners that will spark her imagination and challenge her physically. She often tends toward the more pliant bodies in the room, both in terms of their physicality and of flexibility of mind. In mirroring, people will usually find bodies with whom they are most comfortable partnering. I have learned that intuitive, gravitational choices are best.[3]

When you have a large number of people in one room, it is vital that everyone be seen, both literally and figuratively. Everyone must be able to connect with everyone else in the room in order to accomplish the movement, but perhaps more importantly, everyone must feel that they are a part of the work. In order for that feeling to take root and grow, one must have the sense that others are witnessing his or her contributions. This is both a spiritual and a material concern. Beginning with my experiences as a choreographer in Dance Diner, a leader at LAMD&B, and a teaching artist in schools, I had to learn quickly how to create a welcoming space where young people, older people, all people could feel recognized and present. This is not just a question of emotional attention: this is a question of space and physical orientation. How can I literally see everyone?

It seems obvious, of course—we stand in a circle. The spatial formation of a circle is incredibly powerful. It is a symbol of equality, an assertion that no person stands in front of another, or blocks another from view. It is a commitment, a place where all can be seen and all are equal. Moreover, the circle is a formation that is used in many folk dances, Indigenous dances and choreographies. There is power in coming together in this shape, dancing with a common aim or goal.

Standing in one circle and witnessing everyone in the room is an essential component of Movement Speaks. One should never be behind a person, so we spend time knowing how large a circle to make every class. Shy people often do not like being seen and choose to stand behind another, but even slightly blocking yourself makes for an uneven circle. After the warm-ups led by our teaching artists, we begin with the specific formation of the circle, reminding everyone to stand shoulder to shoulder. This circle is our tool for orienting ourselves in the Passing exercise. As the facilitators, we do not move on until we see that everyone has performed a little bit of the suggested movement because it is important that the group remains together, that no one is neglected or ignored. This is true for everyone's health from a physical standpoint, and also from a more holistic and expressive standpoint. We are in class to be healthy in our bodies and our creative spirits. All movement is good, any body in motion creates good movement—but this movement must be seen in order to be fully expressed by a student. Dancing in the dark does not give you that same sense of self.

In addition to using the circle in the Passing exercise, we also use the shape for help in describing simple choreographic formations commonly used in dance. Circles, diamonds, lines are also used.[4] The sense of where you are and the shape you are making in space encourages structure and clarifies relationships.[5]

When you find yourself in a larger group, note the relationships between people. A person who always leads the line must be clear in determining her leadership. This observation led to another exercise we practice often: Rotating Diamond. A group of four dancers create the four points of a diamond, and they begin to move in that spatial orientation. Everyone faces one direction, and the three dancers behind the tip of the diamond attempt to follow the movement of the person at the head of the shape until at one point they complete the movement and simultaneously turn the same way, over the right shoulder or left side—and in so doing, determine a new leader. In an exercise like this, one has the opportunity to lead and to follow depending on where you are standing and who you

Diamond Dance Formation. Photo © Meg Goldman Photography. In photo: Raeann Bessellieu, Brenda Jones, Sandra Frasier, Judy Rogers.

can see. Students have commented on how difficult it is to lead and how fun it can be to follow. You need to be close to your instincts as leader. You cannot be afraid to move in a new way, both new in the moment and new for your history of movement. Encouraging contrast is the hardest part of teaching, but it is always when you break free of the obvious that the dance gets interesting.

A variation on Rotating Diamonds is a method of movement called Flocking. Flocking is the creation of a spatial formation that dancers use to travel like birds. Again, the main point is to continue moving in the direction and style of those who are visible to you. Maybe everyone is heading downstage on a curve, and then switches to follow someone else's shoulders heading upstage! When performed with precision, all shifting simultaneously or one by one, the movement is incredibly satisfying to watch, even if the action is simply walking.

Again, the movement does not need to be complicated for it to be powerful. Any movement, and any person, when dancing at the top of their ability, can create something powerful. And the power of being seen, generating movement, and the collective witnessing and responding to that movement—it's incredibly inspiring to enact and to observe. To celebrate the artistry, whether evident in complicated or very simple movements, we create large-scale, public dance works in iconic spaces as part of Dances for a Variable Population's mission to promote the visibility of older adults. This visibility does not just impact the older performers but makes members of the audience feel visible as well. These performances are always free of charge—we want to do everything we can to tear down the barriers to entry for dance.

When Dances for a Variable Population performed in Duffy Square in the heart of Times Square in 2014, I was stunned at the amount of people who wanted to try creative movement. This project, called *Roundup* Times Square, was created over five months culminating in five performances. Every person who was part of the project came each day, in their fuchsia tee shirt and black pants, to perform and help teach the audience dance. We created a protected circle bounded by planters in the middle of Broadway between 47th and 46th Street to teach dance. The format was twenty minutes of set performance followed by twenty minutes of a workshop led by older adults who had been taught how to lead the sessions with the larger crowd in Times Square.

Many kinds of people were there, reveling in the physical movements we led them in. Seniors, middle-aged adults, children—the spirit of dance spilled over onto the whole of the space. We broke our bounds. Even more special, the leaders were residents of a formerly unhoused senior center on 43rd Street. Dancing provided a greater purpose, and I was struck by the idea of mastery and skill that dance gives us at any age, in any station of life. People felt spontaneously free to dance, perhaps because they were being led by so many older adults, perhaps because we were so integrated into an open space.

As I build a dance, I think about what can be done, what can be created with each group. As a choreographer, my choices of movements are defined by memory retention, mobility, and fears. I consider what moves are my dancers comfortable making. Dancing and improvising are a stretch for older adults with little training, and it is best to make them as comfortable in performing as possible. The goal is to make them feel safe by giving them choreography they can do with specific places in the music to improvise.

When creating the piece *10027*, my fellow choreographers and I wanted to both create a safe, comfortable space for performers, and at the same time break them out of their own spaces of security. The name *10027* refers to a zip code in Manhattan that has experienced a lot of changes over the years. There are three different housing projects in that neighborhood—middle income housing in Morningside Heights, NYCHA apartments in Grant Houses, and the Manhattanville residencies—that are geographically close to each other. However, people often do not connect to each other across these different housing units. I wanted to create a performance that would foster connections, dancing at five different sites in the zip code and featuring dancers from each of these areas. We then asked the audience to travel with us from one site to another. Even though it is all one neighborhood, many had never ventured passed their own parts of town. We led dancers from an outdoor basketball court to a community gym to a local garden, finishing on the street that connected each site. Although the dancers and the audience members were from different communities that lived in different areas, they were dancing together and seeing the parts of the neighborhood they did not usually see. They were both at home, and not at home. They could find the comfort of the familiar while also exploring the unfamiliar.

In creating *10027*, I considered the balance of the dancers' comfort and discomfort. While building the choreography, I made sure to integrate movements the group could remember, both based on the steps and also where their particular section of the performance took place. One dance was conducted by residents of a housing development on the stairs of their building, an area they knew and felt comfortable performing. I gave them choreography they could remember by relying on the following work we use in class. The dancers would be situated along the stairway, and at the foot of the stairs would be a teacher, someone they trusted well. Then all the dancers could look down the staircase, and simply follow the person in front of them. They were able to follow and perform that pattern with ease and confidence.

As for their costumes, the dancers all felt comfortable wearing different pastel shades that they chose themselves. I had learned the value of self-costuming years prior when selecting clothes for a large group in a public space. We were doing a piece for the new Terminal for the Staten Island Ferry, and I brought in a costume designer who suggested the dancers all wear white. Many refused to wear what she had designed. Rather than wearing the white costumes, we asked the older adults to bring or find their own white clothing. Older adults generally know what clothing looks best on them, and they have lived too long to be convinced to try anything they do not like. Instead, the diverse group of older dancers agreed to wear clothing of their choice in a single, uniting color. Through this decision, they were projecting what they knew about themselves and their bodies and honoring that knowledge.

Dance-Making

I once introduced our work at Movement Speaks to an audience by saying, "As a dance company, we believe there is a dancer in every human being. As you watch the show, think about the dancer inside of yourself." I was speaking at the Jacob's Pillow summer dance festival to introduce a performance of *Fanfare*, a dance that had originally premiered at the Whitehall Terminal for the Staten Island Ferry. The final gesture of that piece culminated in an invitation for the spectators to join the movement themselves—an all-encompassing, overarching manifestation of our vision for the company, and for dance in people's lives. In the center of that dance there is a moment that hovers, fragile as the silk of a spider's web, and suspends time. It was a dance we built for Bianca; it is she who comes to mind when I think of the power of knowing one's own body's limitations, and one's own body's soaring joys.

When Bianca first began coming to class, I knew very little about her. She had trouble walking and molasses-slow movements. I have a vivid memory of Bianca lifting her water bottle to her mouth slowly, cautiously. The action of lifting the bottle to her mouth took an entire minute. Bianca had Parkinson's, I learned, which made it particularly difficult for her to both initiate and cease movement. But there she was, in dance class. Inventive in her use of the space around her, she made gorgeous shapes using the black, hollow, wooden rehearsal cubes we had in the studio. Rehearsal cubes are often used to represent something they need in a theatrical scene, such as a chair or a large rock. But Bianca used these cubes as pieces of architecture to respond to and create shapes against. Using those boxes, she was happy, high above the ground. Her joy in movement was so clear, we decided to build choreography from her actions. As we were putting together ideas for a site-specific performance in the Staten Island Ferry Terminal, I wondered if Bianca could be a part of it, and how we might both celebrate Bianca's natural proclivities as well as acknowledge Bianca's natural limitations in the work we created. It occurred to me that though the choreography would center Bianca as an individual, perhaps

Performance of *Fanfare* in West Harlem Piers Park, 2016. In photo: (*L to R*) Maggie Gavin, Kaitlin Morse, and Bianca. © Meg Goldman Photography.

we could build an ensemble of younger dancers around her as support. What if, I thought, the dancers could physically support Bianca as she danced, lifting her high above the ground and bringing her to the space she was happiest in class. We brought in three younger dancers to work with that idea. The three dancers kept physical contact with Bianca, and the tactile movement and pressure from the young dancers on her skin and muscle guided Bianca and helped her remember where to shift weight and when. The dance developed from a grounded place, with all the dancers on the floor shifting weight between them, and then they began to lift Bianca, gently and almost imperceptibly at first, and then the gesture grew and grew until they lifted her overhead. The effect of this choreography was impactful: powerful and light at the same time. The open and simple expressiveness within everyone fully on display, the embrace of the different bodies and abilities collided into a transcendent piece of art. A suspension of time, a lift of the spirit—during the three minutes Bianca was held aloft in different positions, she seemed to hover outside our normal experience of time.

The environment is essential for this kind of creation—a space that is safe, that is respectful of everyone's bodies, and that believes in the power and expressiveness of every person. It is those dual truths that allow us to create what we create and allow the dancers that work with us to find something that is truly their own, that is truly their story to tell. Safety, however, is not merely physical safety. It is also an emotional flexibility to listen to the room, to listen to the students, to listen to the bodies present and their needs.

I once had a student, Miranda, come into class one day, alight with inspiration. While Movement Speaks is focused on choreography for a group, Miranda insisted on creating a solo piece. I was hesitant, but I continued to listen. Her husband had recently passed, and her dance was to be a tribute to him. Miranda was clear about what she required, down to the particular selection of music. She needed to make something for herself. Something personal and painful and specific. Her dance was to be an expression of her grief.

Through this dance, Miranda created a vision of grief and of joy. The piece was memorable in the way it countered moments of mourning and pain with moments of lightness. She almost cried and laughed with delight as she displayed her feelings through a short solo, a story in movement that defined her life at this moment and in memories from an earlier time in her life. What was immediately important was the fact that Miranda had witnesses as she performed the dance in class for the other students. It felt important for these moments to be shared openly. We could all be in her grief and witness this moment of time. Dance can be a vehicle for an individual's lived experience, and other people are important in dance— they do not need to be a part of the choreography to be a part of the piece. We still connect through one recognizing the other—we recognized the dance Miranda had inside of her. She later performed her piece at a church memorial, extending her reach of witnesses beyond the dance class. Miranda continues to be a regular student in programs at the library and in parks, and she dances whatever she feels, regardless of any directions we may give. She is always herself in her experience of moving.

What is your experience of moving? What speaks to you? I never tell anyone to just go out and improvise—rather, we improvise based on an idea, whether it is a shape, or a dynamic, or sustained floating movement, or the story of a life. We often give directions to individuals or groups of how to make dances so that the structure is clear and provides something to push back against. Sometimes you can find your way into choreography on your own, and sometimes you need a dance form to interact with and respond to. Never be scared or disappointed by using some kind of combination, counts, or familiar steps. That is dancing too. It does not have to be completely new, but it can be completely new! There's space for both things. Let them inspire you to build a dance or use them as an exercise in choreographic movement.

When I teach, I am not aiming to teach people to choreograph. Instead, we use simple choreographic tools to teach older adults to master the language of dance and methods of improvisation to make dance accessible to every body and every kind of learner. We are not training our dancers to become professional choreographers, we are encouraging them to give themselves over to the thrill of dance. As such, our larger, longer dances are created by guest artists who have thought about dance for years, have a strong sensibility about dance, and have a way of working with our older adults that allows for modifications and adjustments. Our teaching artists assist these guest artists and bring to the process a deep understanding of how to adapt for older bodies. But for those that are interested in applying choreographic structures to make dances of their own based on improvisations, there are other tools. These explorations can lead to some exquisite performances.

When Matilda, who taught me the power of picking up your feet, was still dancing with us, we once created a dance for her and a partner built from a story of her name. Matilda was joined by a fellow classmate approximately her age, Jacqueline. Jacqueline was stout in all its ramifications. She had a heavy build and short stature. Where Matilda was long, Jacqueline was round. Jacqueline worked with mobility issues such as extreme tightness, making her as low in flexibility as Matilda was loose limbed. Though the dance was built for partners, each had the same prompt: to tell the particular story of their own individual name.

Initially, this prompt was inspired by need rather than choice. Matilda and Jacqueline were both longtime students, but both still had difficulty remembering movement sequences. This is not uncommon for a person untrained in remembering combinations of movement. We adapted: the sequences needed a form, and we found such a form in movement created from one's name.

The resulting dance was astounding. Both Matilda and Jacqueline were seated in chairs. There was a small space between the two of them so that they could extend their arms without colliding with one another. Music filled the performance space—Bach's Cello Suite no. 1 in G. They both breathed calmly, their eyes closed, their feet planted stably on the floor. And slowly, Jacqueline's hands began to rise, almost as though the music made them move by magic. They floated upward, and her head began to rise as well, following the action of her hands. The movement was slow, suspended. Suddenly, Matilda dropped, folding forward over her legs. A different dynamic was now in play—contrasting speed and contrasting levels. As Jacqueline moved her hands down in an alternating cascade, Matilda pressed her hands together in a prayer gesture and swooped upward, back to an upright, seated position. Matilda held her hands over her face as Jacqueline continued to repeat her cascading gesture. Slowly, Matilda lifted her hands off her face and raised them high above her head with straight arms, her face toward the sky. Jacqueline's repeated gesture transformed into a kind of circular movement of her arms, with a slight bounce in her shoulders. Again, oppositions were at play: as Matilda was making an impressive vertical with her long arms, Jacqueline was working on the horizontal plane. Now and then certain letters were clearly visible—the wide sweep of a C, the curve of a J, the angularity of an L or an N. But there were other times when the movement appeared more poetic or expressive. With their eyes closed—Matilda's face appearing calm and determined, Jacqueline's brow furrowed with concentration and emotion—Jacqueline and Matilda were telling a clear physical story in their minds and bodies. The prompt gave them a structure, a jumping-off point for creation.[1] By encouraging Matilda and Jacqueline to experiment with vague instructions, the prompt allowed them to create a beautiful dance of contrasts.

"I can't make a dance—I know too much." This is what Jackie told me one day in class. In a way, she was right: when compared to her peers, her world was beyond the usual scope of sophistication and artistry. Jackie Ferrara is a known artist—a sculptor, draftswoman, an artist whose creative period blossomed in the 1970s. Even in 2020, at age ninety, she was working on another commission from the New York City Metropolitan Transit Authority to extend her series of mosaic walls on the platforms, passages and stairways of the subway system at Grand Central Station.

I have had the privilege of seeing her artwork: it is precise and particular. She is best known for her pyramidal structures—they have the paradoxical feeling of being ancient, modern, and futuristic all at once—but she has also designed and built courtyards, terraces, and other architectural structures over the course of her career. No matter her exact medium, there is a stylistic link to all her work. A sense of stacked and layered shapes creating a larger whole, an angularity, a delight in abstraction colliding with mathematical specificity. Jackie has been creating, sculpting, and designing since the early 1970s, with remarkable success. Her work has been on display at the Museum of Modern Art, the Los Angeles County Museum of Art, and the Louisiana Museum of Modern Art in Denmark, in addition to numerous public sites and museums throughout the country. Jackie has a profound sense of self. She is aware of what interests her, what motivates her and inspires her. She is in touch with the full range of her artistry and the ways in which she expresses that artistry. In short, she knows what she likes.

When she began coming to class, she was clear that she was there for the exercise. Strength training was useful for her, dance-making was not. She had never had trouble expressing herself creatively; the visual arts provided that outlet for her, not dance. When it came time for the improvisatory and choreographic section of class, Jackie would summarily pack up her things and leave. She was very frank about the whole thing. "I don't like the prompt!" she'd say, and off she would go.

Occasionally, though, there were those magical times that Jackie did like the prompts. I was honored when she chose to stay for those dance-making exercises. Her choices were always interesting, and she was particular about what she liked to do and how she liked to move. We were all struck by her clarity of form and detail of gesture. When Jackie danced, she liked to move in angular shapes, stepping carefully in rhythms that motivated her. She made gestures with her arms, bending at the elbows and stacking her arms as if she was putting blocks on top of each other. When Jackie danced, you could see her sculptures in her movement. The layering, the sharp edges. She danced clear patterns in her steps and the shapes she found in her body, making squares through her elbows and her upper body, creating a box-like topography on the floor. Jackie could be persuaded to explore other dynamics as well. Swirls used for contrast, wiggling used as accents. Jackie once revealed to me that she had once won a Lindy Hop dance contest as a teenager, which did not surprise me. She ultimately loved to practice any dance that was new in quality, as long as it was specific in time and duration. Lindy Hop as a form is both improvisational and particular, and I could imagine her spirit lighting up the room as she danced with a partner in specific steps keeping time with her peerless magnetism. But ultimately, Jackie's preference for moving in straight lines spoke to her preference to straight lines in her artwork and in her world. What was distinct about her, in all areas of her life, shone through in her movement. She danced the way she thought, the way she saw. She even danced the world around her.

Watching Jackie dance out the architecture of her own sculptures, her own internal interests and topography, I became inspired to try more choreographic modes like the Name Dance. The Name Dance was so successful because the choreography was memorable to the dancers, not necessarily for the movement itself, but because of the meaning associated with it. This style of dance-making gave a new kind of framework for recalling steps based on older information—the kind of information that is always accessible, that is second nature—as opposed to brand new action in a less familiar way of thinking. Rather than dancing a name, however, we danced other memories. We began to create forms built from daily routines—a kind of bridge between a cerebral, abstracted idea like one's name to something more concrete, more based in physical reality. Quotidian activities, like cooking or cleaning or raking leaves from the lawn, have a shape. These actions have a built-in muscle memory. Jacqueline, who had danced the Name Dance with Matilda, drank her coffee first thing in the morning, so we built a dance that began that way, with pouring water into a coffee machine, pouring coffee into a cup. As we continued to explore this style of choreography in class, we discovered that movements could grow from anything: brushing teeth, taking a shower, putting on shoes. This kind of dance developed from the movements we do without thinking about them. By harnessing these automatic movements, we were creating more physical mnemonic devices to aid in memory.

While others danced their habits and routines, however, Jackie danced a space. Using her clear, confident way of moving in straight lines and making angles, Jackie danced her artist's loft. In moves reminiscent of her building block sculpture towers, Jackie could remember associating a corner, then moving to a bench, then taking a shower. It was a story that she could follow, a path that could become a dance.

In this instance, Jackie was summoning a particular space in her imagination, but the literal space around you can also be an inspiration for improvisation or choreography. We call this kind of movement site specific, a creation based intimately and explicitly on the environment in which it is created. Site-specific choreography is different from Jackie's dance based on her loft space. While Jackie imagined a specific space in her Loft Dance, the dance itself could be performed anywhere. In a site-specific composition, the dance is so interwoven into the specifics of the environment that it could not be performed the same way should the environment change. It is made for and of the space in which it was conceived.

One afternoon, I asked the students to divide into groups of four or five to create site-specific dance, taking the current space into account in their choreography. To formalize the work a bit, I gave the instruction that the dance was to use two unison phrases (sequences where everyone moved at the same time) and one canon (a sequence with repeated actions). In addition, they must find a still position at the end. "A simple task, a simple concept," I thought. And yet this simplicity yielded something surprising, complex, and full. Jackie was in class that day, and to my delight, she liked the prompt.

Everyone went off to create, and when they returned, Jackie and her group prepared to perform. They began the dance knocking on the walls of the gymnasium in rhythms, a kind of call and response. It evoked a sort of code, as though they were communicating to each other, "Let's begin." They began a unison phrase in which they traveled, following each other, in straight lines. As the dance progressed, two things became clear. First, these lines were not arbitrary—they were using the lines on the gym floor almost as a map. They were bound to the markings for their course. The second notion that became clear to all of us in the audience was an idea that resonated outward from the piece—these people were not simply performing movement, they were using the strictness of the lines, and the constrictions of the walls, as a weight, a limitation, a kind of cage. They were prisoners, locked in cells, moving in unison to reflect an attitude of confinement and restriction. They did some gestures all together, but there was some freedom in their individual movements, a beautiful counterpoint to the strict adherence to the specifics of patterns on the floor, the specifics of the space. They concluded their dance near a column in the gym, each student dancing a canon, moving in and away from the column.

We were mesmerized: mesmerized by Jackie's presence, clearly and meaningfully leading as the group choreographed the dance; mesmerized by the narrative tale that emerged from a basic series of movements, by the use of abstraction to create a resonant meaning; and mesmerized by the way the space transformed before our eyes. The matted walls that we used for stretching in class were bestowed with new meaning by their new use.

Areas of the space that were often neglected now popped out, impossible to miss. Turning an imaginative eye on the space, a space we all thought we knew, opened up limitless possibilities.

Since the occurrence of a global pandemic in 2020, we have all learned that sometimes we encounter limits in ways we do not expect. During the COVID pandemic, possibilities did feel limited. That massive event ravaged our world and left many in a position of solitude, isolation, scarcity, and confinement. I learned at time, however, that limited space or contact does not necessarily mean limited vision. Now and always, it is possible to engage with our imaginations and dream of new ways to encounter our surroundings and ourselves. Regardless of the circumstances, whether you find yourself confined to your home for public or personal health reasons or you simply are seeking an imaginative outlet, re-envisioning one's space can have amazing repercussions. Just as finding alternate ways of moving can help keep our bodies engaged even as they are changing, seeing one's world in alternate ways can help open up areas of our life where we feel stuck or disengaged. Try reading the exercises in this book, then put it down and create something right in your home. Surprise yourself at the possibilities.[2]

One day, encouraged by the idea of site-specific dances, another dancer, Ellen Maddow, brought her group out of our usual gymnasium entirely. Ellen is like that: bold, intrepid, open to the unknown. I had been connected with Ellen for even longer than her time in my class. Ellen's mother, Freda, was one of David Nillo's students in the old Hollywood YMCA in Los Angeles over forty years earlier. She was one of those dancers dressed in black leotards and soft shoes—always in dance clothes, never in gym clothes. Freda was a model of movement at her advanced age; she always led combinations with power. I was surprised when I met Ellen years later as a dancing student at my own company, but it was no surprise that Ellen inherited Freda's fierceness and bravery when it came to movement.

Ellen was a very creative dancer and a leader in the class. I immediately appreciated her openness to all ideas. She had prior experience in the theater world as a founding member of the downtown troupe The Talking Band, a theater company specializing in experimental work. The troupe describes its work as "illuminating the extraordinary dimensions of everyday life," and that is as true of their dramatic endeavors as it is of Ellen's

Winter Culmination Celebration at Central Harlem Senior Center, 2018. In photo: (*L to R*) Candace Tabbs, Ollie Frazier, Simone Coonrod, Coline Chapman; (*center*) Rita Carrington and Shirley Manning. © Meg Goldman Photography.

dancing.[3] She creates completely unexpected dances. Her presence always brought ingenuity and creativity to the class as she shared her particular way of moving and her aesthetic sense of the world.

That day in class, she was clearly inspired. Ellen and her group of dancers left the gym and discovered an upper-level staircase. They returned to the structure of the original assignment—a piece that related intimately to its site, comprised of two unison phrases, one canon, and a held ending—and composed these elements using the intricacies and particularities of the hallway and the stairway within it. Crossing toward the staircase, the dancers started with the benches lining the wall. One by one, they lifted their faces and created an individual movement. Then they repeated moving all together in the same way. Next, the movements were on the staircase. The group traipsed up the staircase, open to the whole gymnasium, and stopped to do a movement of the arms in unison. They each arrived on different stairs, and together they gracefully raised one arm with a bored expression conveying a group spirit so surprisingly unified, and just at the perfect moment when everyone was visible at different levels of the stairs, looking directly at us. They then waved all together, finally, and froze. We were transfixed.

Over the course of my career, between comedy clubs and boardwalks and dance classes in gymnasiums and over Zoom, I have discovered how fruitful it is to encourage people to create dances based off of their environments. Just rethinking how a space might facilitate movement can offer many new possibilities. Learning from my experience with Jackie and with Ellen, I have found that employing the tools of unison movement, canon, and variation of themes can be gateways to allowing for new groups of people to share common decisions and come together, to communicate.

Contact Improvisation

Improvisation does not necessarily mean "invention." Improvisation is not summoning some big idea and trying to fit your body into that idea; rather, it is looking at what is already around you and drawing inspiration from what exists. The power of improvisation lies in noticing. Notice what is there—the specifics of your location, the specifics of your own body—and create something new out of those elements. Contact improvisation adds another element to our list of improvisatory resources. Contact improv lets gravity, and the giving or sharing of weight, open a new pathway to free movement.

I first encountered contact improvisation while studying at Barnard College. I had found myself at a jam session at St. Mark's Church in the East Village with dancers from some of the most important companies in the city. Although I was studying dance at Barnard, the atmosphere at the church was different than any dance environment I had encountered before. There were no pointed or flexed feet, no mirrors, no front prosce-nium, no audience, no choreography even. The form lacked a traditional spatial delineation between audience and performer; everyone in these Jams was a participant in the improvisation. The floor was shared, the role of "dancer" was shared, and most essentially, the idea of center was shared. Recall your mind-body connection—take a deep breath now and recon-nect to your somatic understanding of where your center is. Now, imagine that that center of gravity, that balance of weight, is not only yours but something to discover between yourself and another person. Two bod-ies, in contact, discovering balance in the physical points of connection between them: this is contact improv. It requires an immense trust, and an immense kinetic understanding. There are no pre-determined steps; it is about listening to your partner's body and your own in real time.

I was transfixed by this new dance form. I trekked all over to differ-ent studios and classes and Jams, from Soho to the East Village to the Lower East Side. I particularly loved watching dancers from the Trisha Brown Dance Company do their work: Randy Warshaw, Steven Petronio.

Watching Randy and his partner move through precarious balances and turns of events was mesmerizing. The aesthetic of the form delighted and hypnotized me: the movement engaged the naturalness of the body, the naturalness of gravity, and created a form that felt as organically fulfilling as watching movement in nature—a fish encountering a current, the movements of rushes in the wind. There was a beauty in the visible ethic of the movement; the dance did not delineate between principal dancer, soloist, and corps de ballet. This was a physical manifestation of equality: each participant was necessary to the ultimate creation, each contribution by definition about a striving for balance. These dancers were equalizing the performance of form, dancing with any body and embracing all the parts of that body as valid and essential.

I found the teachings from contact improvisation to be useful in motivating movement. Again, you do not need to invent something on your own—you are responding to something physical in the moment. That prompt can be a living being or an inanimate object. One of the exercises we developed at NYU was a version of contact improvisation to share one's center. Rather than sharing it with another person, however, we used a padded wall. At that time, we held our classes in the NYU gym's second-floor dance studio, a space originally designed for fencing. Most of the wall space was taken up with pictures of fencing champions from the 1940s to 1970s—the professional dancers barely noticed these, but the older adults always did. There was one blank wall in the space that was covered with a soft padding perhaps for wild, swashbuckling fencing maneuvers. We made good use of that wall in our classes. We would invite the older students to give their weight to the wall, to experiment with how they might move along its surface while leaning against it, knowing that the wall would not move. This was a liberating idea to the older adults: the wall gave them information to use in creating movement, without any risk of moving itself. It was liberating both in a mental sense, in terms of having a partner to move with, and also physically. It can be incredibly freeing to pass off your weight.

Weight sharing in this way invites a childlike playfulness into the practice. But weight sharing is only one component of contact improv. A deep element of that style of movement is related to listening and responding. A wall is stable and predictable—our movements leaning against it become the chief source of freedom and imagination, but the wall never surprises us. The wall never gives us new information to respond to. Only a fellow

Slow Soft Touch, Modern Dance Class at Rod Rogers studio. In photo Erika Roth (*center*), Leslie Prosterman, Naomi Goldberg Haas, Jackie Ferrara, and Ingrid Rothbart. Photo © Meg Goldman Photography.

dancer can do that. In order to explore this kind of kinesthetic intuition and listening, I developed an exercise called Slow Soft Touch, which emphasizes the contact element of contact improv. It embraces the power of dancing with another human being, the intimacy of receiving another's energy and the inspiration that closeness engenders but eliminates the pressure of physically supporting someone else's weight. While in contact improvisation, each partner fully supports the other while they improvise movement that relies on their shared weight. In Slow Soft Touch, you never put all your weight on your partner. You respond to your partner's touch, light points of pressure at a slow, clear tempo and this creates your shared movement, rather than the full exchange of weight.[1]

I remember one student, Bella: a frail but feisty dancer who loved working with others. Small, with stunning designer glasses and always perfectly coiffed hair, she was rhythmic and strong, a jumper who would lightly travel across the floor, bouncing. She was inspired by others but careful about what she would try. She was ninety-two at the time, and having lived happily and healthily for so long, she did not want to get injured in dance class. She loved the freedom to move, and while she was careful, she never wanted to be seen or defined as "old."

To work within Bella's limitations while embracing the freedom she craved, we tried creating a dance in class using the rules of Slow Soft Touch. This dance is not choreography exactly, but more of an exploratory exercise. The prompt of the exercise is to be led by touch—you receive an impulse and then respond to that impulse by changing position in relation to your partner and in relation to the room. The exercise concludes by holding a balanced position at the end. Trying different positions that Bella could hold was one part of the exercise, but the other challenge for her was to find new places to be, and then moving to those places smoothly. The surprise of balancing at the end of the dance, knowing the shared weight of a partner, proved interesting to behold. Each dancer was entirely dependent on the other, and this trust created something in real time that could never be precisely imitated by anyone else, and those creative decisions were happening right before our eyes.

The magic of contact improv is that from the perspective of the audience, it is almost impossible to identify where and when an impulse begins. To watch this kind of movement is to watch something ephemeral and paradoxically edgeless. Though the dance is constructed out of two or more people relating to their bodies' surfaces and their mutual weight redistribution, it is almost as though the individual bodies meld together, creating one body with no edges at all.

So much of what we do, at Movement Speaks and in life, is shared through collaborative creation. We all share weight with each other metaphorically—the weight of life that we share with our spouses and partners, the weight of responsibility that we share with colleagues when approaching a project. Contact improv is a beautiful manifestation of a real interaction that we perform daily. The world would be a better place if we were as aware of each other as we are in contact improvisation—if we were as cognizant on the ways we are all dependent on each other to stay balanced.

4

THE GRANDE FINALE

The Art of Change

I have been enriched by the professional dancers, young and old, that I have worked with throughout my career. I am reminded of Stuart Hodes and the fearlessness with which he moved and created. He was a role model for the dancers we worked with for his singular ability to adapt joyfully. Stuart possessed the unique capacity to keep on practicing and embrace change, creating new movements to accommodate his changing body. Stuart once taught us choreography from *Balancing Act*, a routine he built to take care of his neuropathy. A common affliction, and very concerning for a dancer, peripheral neuropathy it is the result of damage to the nerves outside of the brain and spinal cord, which can lead to numbness in the extremities like the hands and feet.[1] For a dancer, losing the ability to feel their feet is a terrifying prospect. Stuart knew the restorative nature of dance and developed a dance for himself to help him feel his feet. The dance was based on the idea of exchanging weight from leg to leg, grounding himself and reawakening the senses in his feet. He shifted weight from side to side—he said it was easier than front to back—on the lateral plane as opposed to the sagittal plane. He would lift one leg and then the other, bend forward to touch the floor, and work himself into a breathless and fatigued state with these movements alone. He shifted weight constantly with rhythm and would end with what he called a creative nonsense monster. Just moving for fun, set to the big band music of Glenn Miller.

Stuart regularly practiced this dance, which he called the *Balancing Act*, along with a daily walk up and down four flights of stairs to get his newspaper. He also performed *Balancing Act* with DVP in front of and with crowds in Washington Square Park, West Harlem Piers Park, and the New York Botanic Gardens. DVP students would perform the piece once with our company and then encore the dance as a participatory excerpt with the audience. Crowds overwhelmingly joined each show. His energy was so infectious, it blossomed on the faces of everyone in the crowd. You could just see the way this dance created joy in addition to good health.

Folks could not get enough of Stuart's magic! At ninety-five, Stuart was still fit and living his life as a dancer.

The way Stuart saw possibility in movement, no matter the obstacle, opened something in people. Watching Stuart be creative and adaptive in the face of challenges truly made you want to grab life and live it. Try the dance yourself, and I imagine you will feel the same.[2] Who would imagine that one could make a dance designed to care for neuropathy? Stuart was unafraid to see his body as it is now, and he celebrated his body. His performance was so powerful, so sweeping, that we all wanted to be a part of celebrating him and celebrating ourselves.

Several students have inspired with their adaptivity, exemplifying the idea that dance is for all people—at any age, and living any lifestyle. Former Martha Graham company dancer Marnie Thomas Wood still dances at eighty-three. As a younger person, she went on tour with Martha Graham's company. Graham told her that she could bring her three children on tour, but at the same time, she removed Marnie from several solo dances. Marnie knows how to modify; she wasn't stuck in her ways or her understanding of herself as a dancer. When faced with a potentially disappointing situation, Marnie simply adapted to continue on dancing. It was important for her to keep moving in the Graham technique, but she also knew that her body had changed; she could acknowledge these differences bravely, and simply say, "I will do other parts." Marnie is still doing other parts, making steps that make sense for her. I admire her beauty when she reaches to the sky with one hand raised overhead; she sings grief, joy, and love in one moment. Her capacity for expression is endless—she understands the power of movement.

Great dancers inspire with the simplest of gestures, even if their dance practice requires a changed approach to movement. The great, masterful NYCB dancer Heather Watts raises her arms in a fifth position and inspires us all to lift in a fifth position. When she stopped performing professionally, Heather took a few months off before turning to swimming at a local gym. She appreciated the effort to continue moving, even if it looked different than what she had been used to. When Heather teaches, she relates her experience to that of her students, congratulating them on their efforts and the accomplishment of attending weekly class. Heather recently taught the opening sequence of George Balanchine's *Serenade* to a group of older adults at a library. She believed that everyone could do the choreography—they could find their way through it, their interpretation of Balanchine's intentions. She was right: they found their own way of dancing, but with Heather's encouragement, that class performed their first tendu ever, stretching their legs to the side in a pointe, a la second position. Dancing choreography to Tchaikovsky required that we use images connecting the movements to meaning—Heather told us, "We're poets! But our words are movements." She encouraged the dancer to connect their movements to the counts, to their imagination of the iconic blue sidelight that inspired the musical piece. She has the most intuitive understanding metaphor—both as a tool, and also a way of life. We must be able to transform, to make connections, to think differently, in order to live happily and healthily.

DVP choreographers can create a sequence rapidly with these older dancers, as they take it on themselves to change the steps to work better on their bodies. Sometimes this method of choreographing is in an adjustment. I think of George Faison, an amazing dancer and choreographer who came out of Alvin Ailey and won the Tony for his choreography in *The Wiz* in 1975. George is a presence. A powerful figure of mercurial nature, he flits between human and seriousness: but his absolute constancy is his celebration of the Black dancer and Black body. It was such an honor when George came to work with us—but also a challenge. George was accustomed to working with trained, professional dancers, while the older adults at DVP were not the seasoned dancers that George was used to.

George had thrilling ideas about basing the choreography around the particular histories of the older adults we would be working with up in a senior center in Harlem. His goal was to create a choreography based on the older dancers' stories of the Harlem Renaissance. He wanted to paint a picture of their youth with the dances they grew up with—creating an imagined landscape grounded in their personal stories.

One the first day of rehearsal, over forty seniors joined. They craved proximity to George and his virtuosity. To see him move and hear him speak was absolute magic. A celebrated figure in Harlem, he had a magnetic pull about him. On the second day of rehearsals, the class had swelled in numbers. Inspired by George's presence and his creative vision, all of the students wanted to take part in his projects. However, it was clear that George was having trouble changing his methods when working with this untrained group. He shouted, "Go down stage!"—an easy enough instruction to those that are used to being on stage and understand that "down" means forward and "up" means back. But these were not seasoned dancers, they were just regular people excited to dance. They became confused and did not understand where to go. George had been right that these adults had plenty of fascinating lived experience in their bodies, but he had not realized the work it would take for them to access that experience through dance.

On day three of rehearsal, the group dissolved to only ten people. Some might look at this as a step backward, but this change turned out to be a gift. With a more comfortable cast size, plus a few older trained dancers, George was able to set the choreography to the music of "The Mooche" by Duke Ellington. There were still moments of difficulty, but rather than be disheartened by these difficulties, George began to simplify the movements and experiment with improvisation. If set moves were challenging for people to remember, do away with set moves! By the time of the performance, George knew that a certain amount of improvisation would be best for this group and allowed space for that. The most important gift he could give these adults was the space to feel comfortable. The process resulted in a glorious dance, filled with stories, personalities, and radiance.

Choreographers must be open to change. One cannot get stuck on one way to do something; one must be in conversation with the bigger idea. A choreographer must have a beginning, middle, and end, a concept large enough to encompass changes or deviations from the initial plan. No matter whether you see yourself as a dancer, a choreographer, or simply a person with a changing body moving along his or her personal timeline, the key to holistic health, wellness, and happiness is an openness to change. This requires a connection to a larger idea, but loosely held. Dance helps us with physical flexibility, which is important, but dance is also important in reinforcing of a kind of spiritual flexibility. This flexibility affects the way you see yourself and the way you move through the world.

I have worked hard for this kind of flexibility, though life continuously throws me curveballs. There are always new changes that threaten to stiffen one's body and mind, make the spirit brittle. I know this intimately. This past October, I turned sixty-one years old. Being sixty-one comes with various changes—change is just part of the deal, the fine print of aging. I have worked with older dancers for some time now, so I anticipated certain physical changes that I have witnessed other professional, older dancers experience. I know that I am no longer the young dancer I was, that I no longer occupy the exact body that I trained and conditioned as a younger person. These changes are to be embraced—I am comfortable occupying these kinds of transformations. But those were the metamorphoses I expected. It is the changes that I did not see coming that I have had more trouble with.

Curtain Call?

"All right everyone, we're going to move across the floor in waltz time. Remember the waltz? It's on a three count, with a big downbeat. *One,* two, three, *one,* two, three . . . got it? OK, let's try it." I situated myself in the room so that all the students could see me. I arranged my body so that I could demonstrate the timing properly.

"Ready? OK, observe me. It's a simple ONE, two, three, and we couple that with our feet. So with the ONE, two, three, we do DOWN, up, up, DOWN, up, up. Watch me."

I began to move. But even though I knew the rhythm in my head, I could not feel it in my body. I felt a dropping sensation in my gut. Something was wrong.

"I'm actually going to step out here. Can one of our teaching artists step up and show the group?"

I stepped off the floor, reeling.

Waltz time was deep in my blood. I grew up singing along to *Fiddler on the Roof,* dancing around the house with my sisters as we crooned, "Matchmaker, matchmaker, make me a match! Find me a find, catch me a catch!" ONE-two-three, ONE-two-three. We created choreography to *The Sound of Music*'s "Edelweiss": "Edelweiss, Edelweiss, every morning you greet me . . ." ONE-two-three, ONE-two-three. The easy rhythm felt like home to me. But suddenly, the lilting rhythm felt like bouncing, like a violent, jerky kind of bouncing that no longer felt right. Or rather, I could imagine the rhythm in my head, but could not physically find it in my body. I stood there, watching my students and teaching artists explore this rhythm, and felt entirely divorced from myself. This rhythmic loss felt beyond explaining rationally, and impossible to explain emotionally. What was happening to me?

As I learned later, after scores of doctors' visits and medical tests, Fahr's happened to me. Fahr's syndrome is a rare, genetically inherited neurological disorder characterized by abnormal deposits of calcium in the areas of the brain that control movement. Four years ago my doctor informed me that I had this incurable condition. Among a litany of symptoms, Fahr's can cause deterioration of motor function, seizures, poorly articulated speech, stiffness of the limbs, and involuntary, writhing movements. More common symptoms include disordered muscle tone and involuntary, rapid, jerky movements. An overwhelming list. When the doctor told me this smorgasbord of potential outcomes, part of me wanted to scream, "But what does this mean for me?" In many ways, as my doctor explained, the symptoms of Fahr's syndrome can resemble those of Parkinson's disease. That was a term I understood, though it sank my heart to hear it. That comparison, and this disease, was a disheartening diagnosis for someone like me, a person for whom movement is at the center of life. As a dancer, this felt more like receiving a death sentence than a diagnosis.

But I was not resigned to this fate. Upon receiving my news, I desperately and immediately sought advice about treatment, asking doctors all across the country about the prognosis. I was determined to find a way to keep moving, to hold onto the motor function that feels so deeply tied to who I am. A curious discovery emerged through these conversations. In an interesting twist, most doctors have told me that my dancing and movement exercises have likely kept the disease from progressing. They added that dance may even have been masking symptoms. For example, my MRI shows such invasive damage to my brain that according to the scans, I should be unable to walk; but here I am. Still standing. Still moving. Still dancing.

The fact that I dance did not make this disease a death sentence. In fact, dancing fought against the degeneration associated with the disease. Dancing was the cure; or rather, the stopgap. I am revealing my personal optimism with words like "cure." I wish the cure were as simple as Just keep dancing. And to be fair to myself and my optimism, I have reason to think that way. At twenty-six, I did manage my diagnosis with lupus through movement. But unlike my experience with lupus, where I was truly able to keep many of the worst lupus symptoms at bay, Fahr's has presented more of a challenge.

I must admit, this part of my life is difficult for me to write about because I wish it were not true. But the process of writing this book has changed my outlook. I wrote this book to inspire movement, any movement, despite feelings of hesitancy, or shame, or fear of failure. And this book is about sharing what I have learned through my experiences over a lifetime of dance. To share this part of myself—this part of me that struggles with the way her body is changing—is also to tell you that when I give you an exercise about lifting your feet as you walk, that exercise is not being pulled from thin air. It is not a judgment from an authority, from the true masters of movement—I do not hand it down to you from a throne. I am not speaking in the abstract; I speak in the personal. I give you exercises like lifting your feet as you walk because I know, through my current experience, how difficult that action is to do. And how important.

Do you remember the series of exercises I developed based on Matilda? Those are exercises that I use every day now. Since I was diagnosed, it has become extremely important to remind myself to roll through the foot as I walk. With this advanced stage of Fahr's, my gait has become less of a stride and more of a shuffle. This is an example of what I mean when I say I am not speaking in the abstract, but rather in the personal: I now understand so many older adults who shuffle. No one wants to think so much about walking. I understand, I certainly do not want to think about walking, I want to just walk. It is crazy that this activity feels effortful to me, that it takes this much consideration. Many of you may relate to that idea—you do not want to think so hard about movement that used to be entirely second nature. But because I understand this line of thinking, I can also tell you with the authority that comes with experience: walking properly is worthwhile. This work we do not want to do is essential. It matters. Your health matters. Shuffling may feel more secure, because your feet never leave the ground, but I am much more secure when I lift and place my foot on the ground, heel to toe. I feel more balanced and more limber. To walk with ease requires this work now: for me, and perhaps for you. We must gracefully accept this change in our lives and do that work. Our bodies will thank us for it.

Grace is sometimes easier said than done, however. Accepting this new change with grace is a daily challenge. This new phase of Fahr's is exhausting. It is tiring to teach classes most days now, and not necessarily in the ways you might expect. For example, I used to pride myself on not having to use a microphone in class. I was no Finis Jhung—my voice was loud when I needed it to be. No matter the context, my voice was heard. I could speak over the volume of music in oversize gymnasiums, I could get the attention of unruly young people as they chattered in classrooms. When I was doing performances in schools, I could command entire auditoriums of teenagers without amplification. My voice, just like my body, felt like me. It did not feel variable, like something that would fade in time. It feels impossible to me to have lost the use of my voice in that way, but here we are. Not only is my speech unclear, but my frozen facial expressions make it an effort to speak publicly. Of course, I do the exercises—this time, in speech therapy. In therapy, I learn various techniques to be more articulate. I take more breaths. I speak more slowly so that I can annunciate words clearly. I approach these tools with grace, but I also know that grace can go out the window in real life situations. I take one figurative step forward and two figurative steps back. Still, I never lose sight of my destination, even though it can now take me much longer to get there.

These moments of frustration remind me over and over that even in my struggle to give students verbal or physical examples, I remain a perfect example for my students. I may not be able to perform the steps the way I used to, but I can adjust. I can find a way for myself to move that feels good, that I can do, even within my limitations. When I hear that old familiar friend, the waltz time, I simply hold the two-three count. Another solution might be to slow the movement down, but not so much that you lose the step. I like to do the big *one,* and then rather than take the two smaller movements on the two-three, I take one more manageable movement and hold there, before the next downbeat. This makes both moving and instructing others in movement more accomplishable for me and has helped me be a better teacher. I offer the suggestions to others that I may need myself. Now in many circumstances, I offer the option to hold the count if a movement feels too fast for some of the dancers. It turns out that many older adults enjoy moving in both ways; they like to sway and bounce, or just to sway only. Both types of movement are fine, what is most important is putting forth the effort and to enjoying moving.

I use the work of dance to regulate my Fahr's from causing me more troubles. I use the exercises noted in this book as often as I can. Every day I tackle pain, set a meter of how I feel, how I am today. I am convinced that the daily work of attention to my alignment and to my energy, attention to making the effort and to the work of the body, prevents my disease from advancing.

My friend Susan reminded me recently of learning ballet and the day-to-day experience and essentialness of a dancer doing a barre. The ballet barre is a daily practice known to all dancers studying the form. When you gather at the barre at the beginning of class, it becomes a time to anticipate, to line up where you are at, to access and assess the day, to come into the present moment, to move into steadiness. It is a time to breathe into the present moment, to notice how you are standing on your legs in this moment, today. When I was first teaching dance, I realized how important it was to have a regular practice, a mental place to arrive every day. I sought to provide my students with some sense of the barre: a reckoning of the day, a time to go slow, tune in, sensitize. To meditate in movement. Creating a regular form of study was necessary. My regular routine was built out of knowing where you begin, having a consistent start and regular progression, like standing and performing plies, and then moving to tendus. I knew that dancers understand the importance of being present through the barre and the significance of flexing that mental and spiritual muscle by accessing this mindfulness every day. Now as I grow older, discovering my frailties, I have understood how vital this practice is to me.

Encore

As I finish the writing of this book, I take a moment to be present. To look at where I am now. Where I am now is a miraculous amalgamation of everywhere I have been. For four years now, I have continued taking yoga classes. I am learning to let my body understand itself and make adjustments, knowing what is possible and comfortable for myself. Along with daily improvisation, yoga grounds me in myself. It offers me a place to try our postures and practice awareness, steadiness, mindfulness. It is my new ballet barre.

I want to do the extreme postures, the extreme steps of choreography requiring fast footwork and rhythms, the balances on one leg, the turns of double pirouettes on pointe. I want to feel the lightness of jumps and the delicious rocks of waltzes, but I know that is not possible for my body now and will never be again. However, I feel the remembering of those postures and rhythms and can perform alterations that allow for those feelings to return. I am forever involved in the investigation of what is, here and now. This is what saves me from despair about my diagnosis and progression of my disease. The diagnosis is a part of who I am; it cannot be changed. It is a disability that affects my mobility but never my capacity to own experiences of movement. I still have the capacity to change. As it has become more difficult to speak, I have trained many teaching artists to be my echo. Now I have a slew of talented creative teachers sharing the Movement Speaks methodology, and this book shares my approach to health in the body. There is always an alternate approach—while the body has limitations, we are never limited to the point of inaction.

A lifetime of dancing has given me lessons for living. I wish for all people to be present in their lives, with the awareness of a dancer. My favorite dance teacher was the English-bred, Pavlova-trained Muriel Stuart, with whom I studied at the School of American Ballet from age nine to twelve. She used to repeat a few words: "Lift up softly, and drop down gently," she would say, lightly touching the dancer's body in the front, under the ribcage, and on the back, alongside and under the shoulders. "Lift up softly, drop down gently." These six words could be interpreted for each individual, as she understood. She led us through balances, waltzes, and arabesques, insisting the musicality was essential to dancing. I seek the joys of musicality, lifting up softly and dropping down gently every day whether I imagine waltzing or mindfully covering ground slowly. Always at my own pace.

Instructions for a Present Ending

We end each class at Movement Speaks with an explicit acknowledgment of gratitude. This is vital. To class, to happiness, to life. Every class concludes with an expression of thanks and a visual check-in. A purposeful

Grateful for being able to reach toward the sky. Photo © Meg Goldman Photography. In photo: Naomi Goldberg Haas.

seeing of each person who was here. Today. In this class, in this moment. Whether virtually or shoulder to shoulder. We formally take a few moments to take stock of the good. To appreciate what is. To appreciate that we can all be here dancing together. The impulse to thank one's teacher goes back years, through the tradition of clapping and curtseying at the end of ballet class or taking a moment to acknowledge the teacher and the pianist for the music before leaving the room. In Movement Speaks, we extend this moment to include all of us—making the moment of gratitude go beyond oneself like in a yoga class and recognizing the activity of all. We are all making the magic moments of dancing because we are all together. If you are dancing by yourself, all parts of the body are talking to each other in order to move as one. The same holds true for dancing as a group. We often make an individual movement one by one, which says both thank you and goodbye in silence, or perhaps accompanied by some meaningful music, like "Farewell" by Polish composer Leszek Możdżer. We all join in the end, taking everyone's movement into our hearts and then sealing it with the other hand over the heart. Often we do a choreographed phrase to the Magnetic Fields' song "Nothing Matters When You're Dancing," a favorite of the classes. With a simple arm movement and touching the other hand and running down the inside of the arm sensing the skin, inhaling all together, and exhaling, taking our hearts symbolically to one another. A way to lift up softy and drop down gently together. A way to be present, to be grateful, and to say goodbye.

Exercise for Gratitude

What you need: an open heart
What's your focus: the beauty of just being

THE STEPS

1. Take a moment then place your hand over your chest and feel your own heartbeat. Feel your "you-ness," your being, your life-force.
2. Be grateful for this moment, this time of movement. All that was expressed through you, for everyone to see. To have a moment to take in all the movement around you.

3. Be grateful for the energy to move. For moving whatever you have moved. Be grateful for everyone else's presence, for inspiring you.
4. Be grateful for this moment. Singular. Never to be repeated again. Acknowledge the specialness. Live in thankfulness.
5. Make one gesture that says all of that. Lift something: An arm? An elbow? A hand? Your soul.

Exercises and Prompts
for Making Dances

Stretching

Stretching is the love of any dancer. Who doesn't want to experience a lengthening of the body and release of muscle tension? Here are some everyday stretches we do to prepare and practice at intervals throughout our session. Remember, weak muscles are tight muscles. Always practice dynamic stretches—stretching combined with movement and breath.[1]

STRETCH 1: HAMSTRING STRETCH

What you need: a sturdy chair and clear space around you
What's your focus: a beginning exercise to lengthen the backs of the legs

Hamstring Stretch. Photo © Meg Goldman Photography. In photo: Charles Macdonald.

Begin sitting down with one leg extended in front of you. Raise the same arm overhead. Fold forward, reaching toward the ankle to stretch the shoulder, lower back, arm, and hamstring. Inhale as you lift the arm high, exhale slowly as you release into the stretch. Repeat with the opposite leg and arm. For stability, remember to hold underneath the chair with your free lower arm. This exercise can also be done standing up for an additional balance component.

STRETCH 2: LOWER LEG STRETCH

What you need: a chair or wall with clear area behind you

What's your focus: stretching the lower legs, the gastrocnemius, and soleus muscles

Start by holding onto the back of your chair or placing two hands on the wall. Step one foot back into a lunge as you drive the heel toward the floor, counterbalancing the torso, head, neck, and shoulders forward in opposition with the back leg. Breathe into the muscle. It is important to feel both hips aligned with your chair or the wall as you lift the lower belly and drive the heel into the ground. Step both legs together and repeat, sending the other leg backward into a lunge.

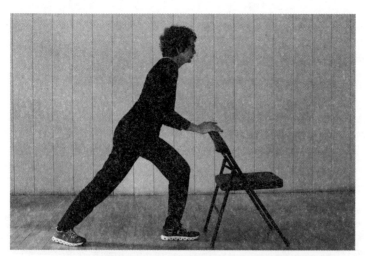

Leg Lunge. Photo © Meg Goldman Photography. In photo: Alice Ellerbeck.

Flat Back Stretch. Photo © Meg Goldman Photography. In photo: Constance Vidor.

STRETCH 3: FLAT BACK STRETCH

What you need: a sturdy chair, table, or wall with room behind you
What's your focus: "back body," arms, and legs (hamstrings)

Begin standing tall with your hands holding the back of a chair or wall or table. Walk slowly backward as your hips and lower back lengthen to form a right angle from the floor or chair or table. Feel the stretch in the back body as your arms reach long toward the wall and your feet press down into the floor. Breathe into the position for five breaths. You can bend and straighten the knees for a deeper stretch of the hamstrings. Roll up through the spine, walking toward chair, to a straight alignment. Sense the length of your body.

STRETCH 4: HIGH BACK STRETCH

What you need: a chair or wall
What's your focus: extending the back body, activating the Latissimus dorsi, opening the shoulders (anterior deltoids), a more flexible spine

After you walk in toward the chair, it is helpful to extend the upper back. Open the lungs with a reverse curve of the spine (after a pelvic tilt), open

Figure 16. High Back Stretch. Photo ©
Meg Goldman Photography. In photo:
Judy Rogers.

the shoulders back with an extension of the upper back. Imagine a foun-
tain shooting upward, cresting over the upper back.

STRETCH 5: SPINAL TWIST

What you need: a sturdy chair

*What's your focus: your mobility of your spine and digestion, overall
health*

Seated Spinal Twist. Photo © Meg
Goldman Photography. In photo:
Sandra Frasier.

Twisting is recommended for your overall health. Practice this at least once a day. Move your spine! This stretch is easy and you can see improvement of the greater rotation achieving more spiral.

Sit in the chair facing forward. Take one hand across body touching the opposite knee and turn toward the direction of that knee. Look over the shoulder you are rotating toward. Remember to keep the pelvis aligned by grounding both sit bones with equal weight. Inhale as you extend the spine, exhale as you increase the twist. Repeat on the other side.

Exercises for Developing the Mind-Body Connection

In these exercises, we will continue our work with the breath from a seated position, and then we will expand to standing exercises using a wall or chair for balance. These exercises are great for beginning dancers, or as warm-ups for those with more experience. I used these exercises when I was recovering from a sprained ankle—they're really great for recovering from an ankle injury, sprain, or tear, as well as being wonderful for general balance practice, strengthening the hips, knees, ankles, and overall body.

General Warmup. Photo © Meg Goldman Photography. In photo: Alice Ellerbeck.

EXERCISE 1: MIND-BODY CONNECTION

What you need: a chair or clear area
What's your focus: breath expansion

THE STEPS

1. From a seated position, reconnect with your breath. Place your hands on your ribcage. Feel the expanding of the lungs and widening along the back.

2. Feel the opening of the muscles of the back and spine line by twisting side to side. Try rocking the body forward and back, side-to-side, over the sit bones at the bottom of the pelvis. See if you can sense the weight of the pelvis and lift of the ribcage.

3. Now let's expand our somatic gaze: we are a body in space, in a room with the ability to move forward and back. Now visualize before moving; visualize standing erect and walking with ease before you begin. This organization of the mind is profound and very empowering.

4. Stand up on your feet. Practice lifting one leg off the ground while at the same time focusing on the drive down, the grounding of the standing leg. Lift one leg, ground the other. Sense the lift of the leg or knee upward while reaching down through the opposite heel of the standing leg—sense the opposition, the causal tightening of the glutes, the engagement of the hamstrings, and quads of the standing leg. This encourages standing upright as opposed to standing unevenly, with one hip dropping lower than the other.

5. Sense all the toes on the ground and across the balance of the foot to the metatarsals, the big toe across to the outside of the heel. Focusing on the standing leg shifts the attention from picking up the foot and worrying about whether you will fall.

6. Stay standing as you pick up one foot and move your head from side to side. Try to stay focused on the opposition—the drive to the ground of the standing leg. Try to move the head from side to side six times. Hold lightly to a chair or wall.

7. Progress with bending and straightening the knee, six times with each leg. Progress with swinging arms to the front and back. For a challenge, try all three together.

Exercises for Balance

In these exercises, we will work on our roots—exploring a wide stance to feel balance and working with a narrower and narrower footprint to challenge that sense of balance. We will work with the mind-body connection and a sense of opposites to find alignment in our bodies, and we will experiment with the ways exercises in balance can also strengthen the hips, and the ligaments of the knees and ankles. These are exercises I learned from Donna who was my student at NYU, while she was at Rusk Institute.

EXERCISE 1: NEGOTIATING BALANCE

What you need: a chair or an empty wall

What's your focus: practicing better balance by finding your center

THE STEPS

1. Stand close to a wall or chair and place your feet side by side.
2. Close your eyes. Experience the small movements of your knees and ankles. Feel the tiny shifts of weight, openly and easily. Do not worry, you have a wall or chair in front of you if you need support. Explore the microshifts in your body.
3. Open your eyes. Face the wall or chair. Close your eyes. Stay in this position for 20 seconds.
4. Open your eyes. Place one foot midway in front of the other with the heel of the front foot aligned with the metatarsal of the back foot. This is called staggered stance.
5. Rock your weight to front foot, to back foot, and back again. Find a comfortable place in the middle.
6. Close your eyes. Find center balance for 20 seconds.
7. Open your eyes. Move the other foot forward and repeat with other leg in front.

Things to Think About

- Balance is easier when you start with your feet planted wide. Think of your weight extending sideways. You want to work with a wide base of support. You're less rocky this way, more stable.

- To increase your steadiness, weight trainers often suggest opening your legs to achieve a wider base of support.
- Touching the feet together is more unstable, but an important sensation to feel. This has nothing to do with age; it is just the nature of physics.
- To create proper alignment, think about a line through the center of your body, going all the way down from the crown of your head, through the back of your throat to your pelvic floor between your legs. This is called the central axis.
- Think about the spine inside the body, as opposed to on the back of the body. This can help you create length.
- There is equal energy moving downward into the floor using the sense of the legs driving through the heels and upward toward the ceiling through the hips and pelvis and the front of the body.
- Remember, at the end of the day, balance is just an ongoing negotiation.

You've been doing it all your life—it's an old friend, make sure you stay acquainted.

EXERCISE 2: BALANCE FROM HIPS

What you need: a clear area with a chair or empty wall

What's your focus: muscles of the hips (adduction and abduction, gluteals, hip flexor, abdominals), strengthening for ligaments of knees and ankles

THE STEPS

1. Face a chair or the wall. Use your left hand to hold onto the back of the chair or press your left hand against the wall. Lift your left leg to the side while lifting your right arm. Sense the opposition of weight—the equal and opposite energy.

2. Try to take your hand away from the chair or wall. Try to re-find balance by extending your leg and arm with equal pulls of energy. Find the center pull of action or central axis.

3. Feel lifted in the standing leg. Keep your hips level. Feel the energy going both ways through your head and through the floor, even as you

Counterbalance Leg Lift.
Photo © Meg Goldman
Photography. In photo:
Sue-Wan Sun.

explore the side-to-side. Feel both energies at once. Feel the sides of the body.

4. Hold your balance for 10 seconds. Keep the arms extended to the side—reaching away from the leg.

5. Prepare to perform this exercise front and back, reaching the leg behind. This will activate the lower back, then the glutes, and then the hamstrings. Extend back off the floor while extending opposing arm in front.

6. Feel the lift of the front of the body extending to the hand. Reach the arm front and up, sense the weight and forward action of the body. Imagine the weight of the lifted leg behind. Reach the leg behind and the arm forward. Take both hands off the chair or wall. Balance for five seconds.

Things to Think About

- You can use music to find counterbalance in time. Practice an arabesque!
- You can use a phrase of eight counts to perform the lift and lower by the end of the phrase. Close with your feet in first position, parallel, with your toes and heels in line, turn out (rotation from your

thighs). Begin again with the opposite arm and leg on the sagittal plane (arm in front and leg in back). Do this 10 times for each leg, changing each time.

- Doing a series of leg lifts using opposite arms can be helpful in understanding the idea of counterbalance. Focusing on equal and opposite sides of the body while strengthening the hip flexors and abdominals along with activating balance on one leg. Music is helpful, encouraging you to step in time while you lift the legs and cross the midline. Touch your hand to the knee at first gradually moving to the elbow to knee using more abdominal strength.

- You can use a bent knee when stepping for a juicy, more fluid workout.

- You can use a similar exercise that can be practiced by either opening the hips using arms to the sides, touching elbow to knee on the same side; or, using the waistline and activating the obliques, while moving on one leg, drawing elbow to knee. This side-to-side motion is very pleasing, as you can imagine a happy baby lifting one leg, and then the other. First practice in front, moving the arms and legs to cross the midline, and then move to the sides, activating the waist, or obliques.

- The counterbalance is more front-to-back than side-to-side. Kicking your legs front while reaching back. Sensing the back body through the arms is also another way to feel counterbalance.

- Even just feeling the back body energy as you lift a leg front is an awareness to focus on. The weight of the leg in front counters to sensation behind even if you do not literally move your arms to the back. Practice lifting your right leg forward and thinking about the solid sense of the back body. Change your legs each time.

- Hamstring curls (i.e., lifting the leg behind you, toward the glutes, while stepping forward) activate the back body while strengthening the balance on one leg. Perform a set of eight repetitions on the right leg and then repeat on the left leg.

- For a cardio workout, move into a series of hamstring curls while crossing the space, with music accompanying your travels.

EXERCISE 3: FINDING ALIGNMENT

What you need: a clear space

What's your focus: your own sense of touch on your body, an experience of widening the back of the waist and closing the front of the body, narrowing the pelvis, zipping up the belly, lifting the sternum, broadening the collarbone

THE STEPS

1. Close the front of the pelvis, widen the back of the waist. Create a circle closing in front of the iliac bones in the front of the pelvis.

2. Sense the ribcage closing in front. Lift from the midline to the manubrium, the center of the sternum. Broaden the collarbones, imagining the shoulders wider than they actually are.

3. In order to really feel these sensations, trace these areas with your hands. Physically move your hands along the lines of your body to close in the front and widen in the back. Stand with your feet parallel, heels and toes in line. Center the weight of the feet to sense the outside of the large bone of the heel crossing to the big toe mound and draw a line of energy up the inner thighs toward the pubic bone.

Exercises for Mobility and Flexibility

EXERCISE 1: PELVIC TILT

What you need: a blank wall or sturdy chair, a clear area

What's your focus: the release of the lower back, mid-back, shoulder opening, the quadratum laboris

THE STEPS

1. Begin with contractions of the pelvis. Then use your mind-body connection to picture this movement in our mind's eye first. This movement connects us with the forward tilt of the pelvis, and an understanding of our head and tail.

2. Work with a rounding of the back body—stretch the upper back and rounding the lower back to open up the lumbar curve. In this way, you are

controlling your weight moving forward, with an understanding of how the spine can open and expand. Ultimately, the spinal processes expand with the movement.

Round Back. Photo © Meg Goldman Photography. In photo: Brenda Jones.

3. Feel that expansion in the back, as opposed to a closing of the belly. The deepest part of the curve is the absolute middle of the back, the belly button reaching back with as much forward strength of the shoulders and lower pelvis. We are exploring, and hopefully beginning to understand, the curve of your own body.

4. Interlace the fingers in front of the belly button. Reverse the hands and press away forward from the body, curving your arms to the front of the space.

Side Back Stretch. Photo © Meg Goldman Photography. In photo: Betsy O'Neill.

5. Now, lift your right elbow and peek under your arms toward the right. Then lift your left elbow, and lightly twist to peek left under that left elbow. Come back to center and stretch into the curve. Raising the arms overhead, push your hands high toward the ceiling, and stretch through the length of the back, feeling the side body as well as the length of the spine line. Remember to connect to the energy pulling down to the floor through the line of the spine and the tailbone, and simultaneously the energy pulling up to the sky through the crown of the head.

Things to Think About

Some bodies are made to experience this sensation: the awareness of the curve, the forward tilt of the pelvis balanced by the weight of the shoulders and the pressing backward of the belly. Others are not, no matter how hard you try. Just like I gravitate toward ballet because it feels best in my body, so too do some bodies gravitate to some movements more than others. While these exercises are very popular, due to the degree to which the back body is activated, I have seen many less-than-effective approaches to these movements; the most common practice is the student who stretches only her shoulders, never activating the lower back, fearful or unaware that she can curve the tailbone anteriorly forward. I less frequently see the student whose back is super mobile and has difficulty organizing her shoulders to align with equal strength forward, sensing the opposition. Be mindful that you do not overstretch your lower back.

EXERCISE 2: PORT DE BRAS

This is another exercise for mobility that stems from ballet—the teaching of a port de bras that Gelsey Kirkland first taught me about.

What you need: a mirror, space for your arms to reach

What's your focus: developing a connection to where your arms are in space

THE STEPS

1. Visualize the heart in the palm of your hand. Wherever your arm is placed—the side, over your forehead, behind you—one should always be able to draw a line to your heart. I extended this idea, asking the

older adults to experience the sense of expression illuminating from the hand.

2. Bring your arm in front of you, level with the heart, and open it to the side. Again find the connection to the heart, allow the body to sense that connection and muscularly feel the placement of the arm.

3. Allow for the latissimus dorsi and deltoids to support the arm. Engage a sense of moving the arms from the core body feeling connected, not raising the shoulders up (words from my favorite teacher at SAB, "*Lift up softly, and drop down gently*"). Owning a sense of where you are in space. This practice creates a very real sense of the body.

Things to Think About

Mobility and flexibility can mean many things. Sometimes, we need mental flexibility—a willingness to try new things, to change our minds, to get to know ourselves and our bodies in alternate ways. And to accept lessons from unexpected teachers, like I did when I learned to "let it go" and move loosely. Mobility and flexibility are also exactly that—physically moving loosely. Loose movement is fast, while tight movement is weak and slow. With tight movement, you can feel something stopping you—and again, this stoppage can be mental or physical, or both. You have to release your body and mind in order to move freely. You have to relax in order to move freely. You also have to have support, which takes us to our next foundational key to dance—strength.

Exercises to Build Strength

EXERCISE 1: ISOMETRICS

What You Need: a wall or chair
What's Your Focus: strengthening the arms, chest, abs, legs

THE STEPS

1. For adduction (from your midline to your center): place your hands inside the knee and push legs against the hands. Work isometrically (using your own body weight to strengthen), push the legs out with the muscles of the arms. Cross your arms to allow for more effort and sense the internal work of the inner thighs as you. Push against the arms. Feel the

strength of the shoulders pushing out as you push in. Sense the strengthening of the muscles of the chest as you lean forward with a straight spine.

2. Place the knees again hip-width apart. Lean forward on an angle and push in isometrically as you move your legs out. Activate the outside muscles of the hips, the shoulders, the pectorals as you lean forward. Feel the front of the shoulder—the anterior deltoid—and the pectorals, the major muscles of the chest.

Adductor Strengthening. Photo © Meg Goldman Photography. In photo: Raeann Bessellieu.

3. Practice a wall push-up: place your hands on the wall, fingers pointing straight up, with your elbow easily placed under the shoulders. Do 10 repetitions of a wall push up in this position.

Wall Plank for Upper Body Strengthening. Photo © Meg Goldman Photography. In photo: Constance Vidor.

4. Repeat a set of 10 with elbows pointing out to the sides, hands remaining parallel with the shoulders, fingers pointing diagonally inward, for an expansion through across the upper back and a stretch in the deltoids.

5. Lastly, do a set of 10 with the arms in close to the body, hands lower on the wall (parallel with the chest or armpits), fingers pointing straight up, and elbows pointing to the ground. This strengthens the triceps.

6. Support your body on a plank board for 10 seconds, encouraging your pelvis to maintain a line parallel to the floor which supporting your abs, strengthening your core while holding your body straight.

7. Finish with a flat back stretch (page 149), stretching your shoulders and legs by pulling back to a right angle bending at the hips away from the chair.

EXERCISE 2: PICKING UP YOUR FEET

What you need: a clear area to locomote

What's your focus: the parts of the feet, awareness of balance connecting to vision, the bending of the metatarsal

THE STEPS

1. Be aware of how your feet touch the earth. Try not to walk with "block" steps; pick up your feet and bend the foot. Place the heel first and roll through the ball of the foot. Keep your knees slightly bent and roll from heel to toe.

2. Practice this walk: stepping from one side of the room to another, rolling through the foot, consciously placing one foot directly forward and then the other.

3. Do not be concerned with placing heel to touch big toe but be concerned with walking a straight line, not drifting side to side. Concentrate on walking directly rolling from heel to metatarsal, bending the foot, the ball of the foot, with each step.

4. After a couple of crosses back and forth, add a turning of the head to the side and using focus to one side of the room and then the other. You can take a couple of steps looking one way and then change to look the other side. Change the focus with alternating steps each time.

5. Next time keep the eyes fixed on one point in front of you and turn the head side to side without moving the eyes, just the head. Use the eye muscles and the muscles that strengthen balance. Very challenging!

Things to Think About

You can progress to using an extreme lift off the leg as you take each step strengthening awareness of using the hip flexors lifting the leg to a right angle with every step. Adding the side-to-side head turn and walking a straight line directly forward. Use opposite arm to the leg, swinging forward from the shoulder and turning the head with the direction of the forward arm.

EXERCISE 3: PICKING UP YOUR FEET, LUNGE VARIATION

What you need: a clear area to step front, side, and back
What's your focus: quadriceps, glutes, abdominals awareness, hip flexors

THE STEPS

1. Engage in a series of lunges with forward steps activating the quadriceps. Change the levels of the body from upright to lowering with every lunge. Balance will be activated as well.

2. Think about the stability of the core as you place the leg each time you step. Think about the heel to glute connection linking the balance of the leg to the core strength. Pushing off of the leg behind with an awareness of the front leg heel to glute connection as you transfer weight. Sensing the lowering of the body from the center level with an awareness of the front to back action, the up and down, strong core and weight equally balanced.

Things to Think About

One way to build support in the body is by doing regular hip flexor strengthening, quadriceps strengthening, and ankle mobility exercises. All parts of the lower body need work, but of prime importance are the quads and hips. Exercises like the ones we are about to work through were extremely helpful for students like Matilda, trying to build strength and "pick up their feet."

EXERCISE 4: FOR HIPS AND LEGS

Strengthening Hip Flexors. Photo © Meg Goldman Photography. In photo: Alice Ellerbeck.

What you need: a clear area to extend arms and legs front, side, back; a chair or wall for support, a steady beat for accompaniment, and a speaker to play music

What's your focus: strengthening of quadriceps, glutes, abdominals, hip flexors, hamstrings, hips (outer and inner)

THE STEPS

1. To strengthen the hip flexors, raise one knee to hip height at a right angle, keeping your hips level. Remember to "pull up" on the standing leg. Now lower the raised leg. Repeat this complete motion six times: six knee-raises to level of the hip at a right angle and rest there, holding each lift for two counts, and the last one for four counts. This is one set. Repeat this set three times for each leg.

2. Front leg extensions: lift a straight leg forward and hold for two counts.

3. Sense both legs straight. Do not tilt pelvis forward with leg. Sense an upright spine and core, and make sure to keep the hips level. Sense the

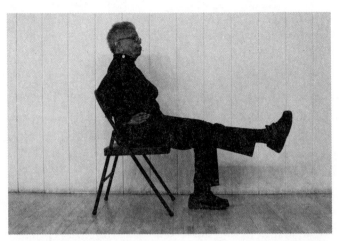

Seated Quadriceps Strengthening. Photo © Meg Goldman Photography. In photo: Judy Rogers.

vertical line lengthening as you close and lower the leg, using the glute of the working leg and connecting to the heel.

4. Imagine you are growing taller as you lower the leg and pull up on the standing leg. Flex the foot, toes to the ceiling. Perform this action six times, and then repeat another set.

Things to Think About

You can lean deeper into the exercise by progressing to a more fluid motion. Brush of the leg out in front of you, pointing your toes, and extending the leg in front with a rhythm and no holds. Doing this six times will strengthen the quadriceps and quadriceps tendon above the knee, which can protect you from knee pain. If you would like to work your hip flexors and front leg extensions seated, the two exercises (below) are great alternatives.

Alternative 1

Distribute your weight evenly on the sitz bones. Now, lift one knee at a time. Try not to tilt or rock side to side—feel level in your hips. Perform a set of 10—five on each side—then rest and repeat. Keep the spine line straight and sense the verticality of the length of the spine grounded to the evenness of the pelvic floor. Imagine the space between the pubic bone and the tailbone in order to sense the pelvic floor. Finish with marching rhythmically, swing your arms, stamp your feet, and encourage impact.

Alternative 2

To do seated front leg extensions, send your leg directly to the front and hold it there with a flexed foot for two counts. Change legs and repeat. Make sure you do not collapse your spine or torso. Keep extending tall.

For Adduction of the Muscles of the Legs

Hold onto a wall or chair. Pull up energetically on your standing leg. Lift the working leg and hold it straight in front of you (imagine a line and cross your leg over that line, feeling this in both inner thighs). If you feel both inner thighs, you're doing it correctly; you're not dropping the standing leg. Really keep the hips level. Do not drop the hip of the standing leg.

Toward center: use both legs in this action. Watch the pelvis staying level and watch the tendency to drop into the standing leg sliding the hip down. Lift up as you cross the working leg 10 times. Then use the other leg and repeat both sides.

For Abduction of the Muscles of the Legs

Abduction means movement away from the midline of body. Lift your standing leg and move your working leg to the side, away from the midline. Flex strongly, sensing the outside muscle of the leg, the outside of the heel, and medial glutes. Resist the urge to move into the quadriceps and turn out the leg with the toes facing the ceiling—have the toes face forward to sense the side of the leg. Do this 10 times with the right leg, and then 10 times with the left leg.

Repeat. Keep the waistline long and the hips level. This will build stability in the hips, and strength of the legs and core.

Exercises for Proprioception

EXERCISE 1: CULTIVATING ONE'S SENSE OF SPACE

What you need: a clear area all around you, whether you are seated or standing; a variety of music from classical, to folk, and R&B, and a speaker

What's your focus: your imagination, and physical sensations

THE STEPS

1. Begin by stretching out into space, explore your limits. It's a luxurious reality to feel reach—to encounter the maximum length of your limbs, your arms and legs—and it is also a key touchstone to understanding proprioception.

2. Swing your arms, up and down, then out and around your body. Create different shapes with your arms: direct arches, curvy pathways, straight lines. Move your arms in these different shapes over your head and around your waist.

3. Explore the idea of near and far space close to your core, up and down your arms, and under and over your legs. Follow your focus with your eyes. Sense the difference between following your hands close to your body and then beyond your body, seeing the far corners of the room. Can you project space beyond yourself?

EXERCISE 2: SPATIAL AWARENESS THROUGH LUNGES

Lunge exercises are both significant strength builders and also are useful tools in developing our concept of space. This exercise is done in sequences of all different directions and incorporates arm movements, challenging us with combined actions and multiple points of focus: twisting and stepping, shifting weight and moving. Remember, when lunging backward, look where you are going!

What you need: a clear area to step front, side, and back

What's your focus: quadriceps, glutes, abdominals awareness, hip flexors

THE STEPS

1. Lunges to the front. Step forward with your right leg, with the back heel of your left foot lifted. Sense your weight shift to the front foot and the heel, without losing awareness of the right leg (the leg you are moving from). Feel your weight distributed equally between your front heel and the back ball of your foot. Your core is strong, belly firm. Create a sense of lengthening through the spine and back. Return to a standing position, and then repeat with the opposite leg. Alternate back and forth 10 times. Hold for one breath. If you want to develop strength, hold the front lunge for a few more breaths. Strength also comes through repetition.

2. Lunges to the side. Lift the knee to increase the awareness of picking up your feet. Try to lift your knee all the way to the height of your hip, and then step to the side. Keep the standing leg firmly balanced, straight and strong. Push off the working leg from a bent knee to the side to return to a legs together position. Sense the weight of the standing leg grounded. The pull of the leg toward the standing leg is the point of balance. One has to push through the standing leg into order to alleviate the pressure on the knee of the working leg. Repeat a set of 10 on both sides.

3. Lunges to the back. Stepping to the back, you must first be aware that is the motivation even from your initial position of straight alignment. Surprise is never an option—know you are stepping back before you start and visualize that action. Keep the front heel grounded and shift weight to the working leg behind. Step back with arms at sides and core firm while looking where you are stepping.

4. Gradually increase step width, holding firm with both legs and sensing the front and back legs bent. Lift your arms overhead as you step back and turn your head to see behind you, finding balance and solid strength. Repeat 10 times.

Score for Pavane Section from *Looking in a Fishtank*

VARIATION FOR ANYONE

1. Decide on two ways to cross the stage in a locomotive repeated movement. This is completely your individual choice. The only rule is that you must move from stage left to stage right and then back again with a second choice.

2. Cross horizontally in two directions toward stage right and again toward stage left using another kind of stepping pattern.

3. Know that at any time you could drop and roll on the floor (share one common move of doing a log roll), continuing in the same direction of your cross.

4. If someone is in your path, acknowledge them in some way, let a movement or encounter happen between you two. End the movement by one of you dropping and rolling horizontally off stage.

5. Use repeated steps and be aware of who is in your path, look out for encounters. Do not step too close to everyone else.

A dance will happen because you are there in this moment. Everyone is repeating the log roll the same way. You are seeking connection.

VARIATION FOR TRAINED DANCERS

1. Enter from one corner of the stage and create an energetic cross in solo, one by one.

2. Enter again but stay onstage and meet other dancers.

3. Develop ideas in one area.

4. Partner and make trios.

5. Move toward a center shape and hold ending.

6. All the while, respond to the music with delight!

Grande Finale Dance

The ideas listed are only suggestions. As an exercise, create the steps to your own *Grande Finale*. The *Grande Finale* dance is learned and performed with each group crossing on a diagonal or horizontally. All should be following each other (do not need to be directly behind one another).

THE STEPS

1. Teach group to learn a battement front. A battement is a kick with a straight leg traveling forward. As you move forward, hold arms to the sides.

2. Teach group to chassé—as you travel, sweep your arms overhead again and again.

3. Teach group to waltz—a 3/4 bouncing step—Down *up up* down *up up.* as you move, sway your arms left to right, and back again.

4. Ask group to travel on their tippy toes. Use a ballet port de bra when crossing—for example, lifting the arms overhead in a circle shape.

5. These crosses can be repeated as many times as desired, or as the music allows—but they should be performed at least twice to give all a chance to dance a second time.

6. Ask group to make a low shape together—perhaps connected—can also put in solo moments or a big sweep of a circle performed by all.

7. Finish with making a clump, using the same dynamic to find a position close together. Find a high shape with arms lifted. Hold the ending.

Some Lessons from Venice Beach

THE BACK RACK

What you need: a soft, flat surface above the ground; it could be a bed, a bench, a low-back chair, or even another body you can lean against

What's your focus: opening the pectorals, chest, and torso

THE STEPS

1. Hanging torso and shoulders over the edge of a bed, experience the sensation of letting go, the opening of the fronts of the shoulders, the ribcage, upper back and arms. The exercise can also be done in a chair.

2. Breathe into the position, enjoy the sensations arising up and out.

Seated Back Rack. Photo © Meg Goldman Photography. In photo: Brenda Jones.

THE PULL

What you need: a stable structure you can hold on to, such as a park bench or a doorframe

What's your focus: opening up muscles along the spine

THE STEPS

1. Hold onto a park bench or stable support such as a doorframe.
2. Bend your knees and pull away from the bench or doorway frame.
3. Make a curve of your spine, rounding your back.
4. Open up the back body. Enjoy the balanced stretch.
5. Tilt sideways and increase the pleasure.

LEG SWING

What you need: something solid you can hold on to, such as a table, a chair, or a counter

What's your focus: using legs in a swinging motion

THE STEPS

1. Stand tall on one leg and swing the other leg to the front and back with a bent knee.
2. Be sure to drop the weight of the working leg as you swing through center, brush the heel on the floor.
3. Bend the swinging leg to an "attitude" front and "attitude" back. Focus on the release and stretch of the hip and working leg (the leg that is moving front to back).

Exercises for Movement Conversations

EXERCISE 1: MOVEMENT CONVERSATIONS

What you need: a partner and space between you

What's your focus: constructing a dialogue of shapes, a conversation in movement

A Duet Using Slow Soft Touch. Photo © Meg Goldman Photography. In photo: Betsy O'Neill and Joyce Steinglass.

THE STEPS

1. Start by using one shape, one gesture, or one movement toward partner. Physically enact a kind of greeting. Hold the gesture for several seconds.

2. Partner responds in movement, beginning a "conversation."

3. First partner creates a new movement and holds. Second partner responds with another movement of the same length or speed, or makes a completely different choice. The second partner should not "talk" or move over the first partner.

4. Progress to making a dance by exchanging movements back and forth. The dance can be very expressive, or partners simply create the next gesture by making an oppositional movement. For example: higher or lower in space, faster, or slower.

5. Try "talking" longer than a short "Hello, how are you?" To expand to a fuller expression, try two or three gestures.

6. Use varying music to make your dance. Try counting 10 gestures, back and forth.

7. Let the dance become fluid. What is important is to watch and feel your partner. See what they come up with!

EXERCISE 2: FOR LARGER EXPRESSION AND COMMUNICATION

This is a modification of the Movement Conversation exercise that incorporates multiple people, perhaps standing around in a circle.

What you need: more people, bigger space

What's your focus: sharing movement with a group

THE STEPS

1. One person makes a statement, dances or moves by herself and ending with directing her shape toward the next person in the circle. She holds her last shape until the next person is finished dancing.

2. She switches position for the third person or picks up new movement dancing again—creating a conversation.

3. The conversation goes round a few times.

Things to Think About

A benefit of this version is that you strengthen physically as you hold positions, and you get ideas for movement by watching your partner(s). Memory is not challenged as all movement is instinctual and improvised. Again, you can respond to what is stated, but really watch and don't talk over your partners.

Exercises for Beginning Improv

EXERCISE 1: LETTING THINGS UNFOLD

What you need: only you

What's your focus: the natural unfolding of a movement or movements

THE STEPS

1. Begin very simply, only moving one hand. Begin with the fingers, spreading them wide, or wiggling them, or opening and closing your hand. Explore this for a while.

2. Extend your attention to the whole hand, the wrist. Move the hand softly from side to side, up and down.

3. Move the hand across the body and back. Now from high to low.

4. Play with different combinations of all these movements. Keep exploring everything the hand can do in space.

5. Now progress to traveling in curves, way up to the sky and down to the floor. Focus beyond the fingers into the larger space.

6. Start incorporating the other hand and initiating new movements. Try moving both arms—move both arms symmetrically and then asymmetrically—one arm up, one arm down, one arm in curves, one arm in straight lines. Soften and see how softly you can move.

Things to Think About

- Let your gaze and attention be a part of your improvisation. Look at your body parts, your shoulder, your elbow, your wrist, your leg, then beyond. Progress to moving your whole body, exploring angles and curves. Continue to follow your eyes—your attention and interest—different places. Whether you are moving and responding to music with a rhythm, or moving without music, follow the pleasure of moving at this moment. In time, in space, within this time, within this space. Take up room. You are announcing your presence, your being. Stretch, twist, expand, melt, in new ways! Look where you are!

- Select a piece of music to play along with your movement—but this time, begin thinking about how you might use dynamics to purposely move against the music you chose. Maybe contrast fast, energetic music with the dynamic of floating.

- Perhaps play slow music, and move in a striking manner, using single strokes of action.
- Try bouncing to an infectious beat at a middle tempo.
- Try "chopping" with your arms and legs to an indiscernible beat and create the timing of the movement with your actions. The action can surprise you.
- Change to embody a sense of striking. Strike forward with your arms. Two arms, one arm high and add your focus. Strike with your leg, your foot, your head. The feeling of moving is very direct, has a focus that is emphasized when you embody that idea. Striking high and looking up is very different than striking low and beyond yourself. Experience the stopping action of a striking movement.
- Moving into a popping action of the wrist, an isolated body part, maybe a knee or foot, an arm, two arms, the whole body popping like popcorn. The movement is direct and quick, unexpected, surprising.
- Experience continuous movement with a sense of weight making curves. Try and come to places of holds in round shapes. Carving actions, sweeps that are direct and end actions, to the sides, in front of you, in low space, above your head, high space.
- Change to expanding your body, wide and high, extending all limbs, changing to contracting like a small ball and pushing your limbs out imagining your bones were reaching in all directions.
- Use your breath to support the movement. Inhale as you expand, pop suddenly and drop as if a balloon took your expansion away then slowly exhale and get smaller.
- Sway side to side, swinging front and back using your head and legs, sense the head tail connection of a full body swing. Can you swing a body part, say just your arms, your head, one leg, both hips?
- Can you move in syncopated ways? Actions that emphasize rhythm and stop movements?
- Can you find places of stillness that you can hold in different shapes? Maybe a tilt? One leg lifted with support? In a curve? Using twisted arms? Straight legs and angles?

There are countless dynamics to play with—the possibilities are as boundless as your imagination. Some of my favorites include swinging, slicing, carving, folding, flicking, gliding, wiggling, twisting, contracting, expanding, spiraling, widening, narrowing. What might happen if you choose three of these words and craft them into a sentence or a poem? Cycling through, you may find that you have created a dance.

EXERCISE 2: MIRRORING

What you need: a partner, space
What's your focus: the movement of your partner

THE STEPS

1. One partner performs a movement while the other partner "mirrors" the movement. Go slower than you think possible and move as fully as you can imagine. Start with a body part that is accessible for movement: a hand, an arm, an elbow, a head.

2. Play beautiful, inspiring music and respond to the music in the movement. Be a leader asking your partner to mirror you. Perform for a few minutes and then switch roles. Sense whether it is easier to lead or follow.

3. Change up the music. Use different movement dynamics and directions: up/down, fast/slow, sustained gliding, and choppy stuttering. Do not forget the face muscles, shoulders, core body.

4. Evolve to standing and lateral movements of the legs and arms. Use distance far and near.

Things to Think About

Experiment with different music. See how the music guides the change of movement. At first, be clear who is leading and who is following. Then enjoy switching the leader without this clarity.

EXERCISE 3: FOLLOWING

What you need: a partner, open space

What's your focus: following with your body rather than your eyes. This is a more challenging exercise, as you are not facing your partner.

THE STEPS

1. Have your back to the person who is following you. The person in front is the leader. Travel through the room maintaining this relationship.

2. Encourage "levels" in the traveling action: different dynamics, different responses to elements around you, like different pathways and actions that move high and low.

3. Change the lead when the person in front (leader) turns toward the person in back. The person in front has now become the follower, and the person who was in the back is now the leader.

EXERCISE 4: PASSING AN IMAGINARY BALL

What you need: a group, space large enough to form a circle

What's your focus: your kinesthetic response to another's movement and energy

THE STEPS

1. Start with an imaginary ball of a particular size and weight. Play with it and share the "kind" of ball with a partner. Partner receives ball as it is given and can change the weight and size.

2. Throw it up, bounce it down, pass from hand to hand.

3. Experiment with different ways of passing to yourself and to your partner.

4. Change the type of ball. For example, move from imagining a basketball to imagining a beach ball to a golf ball to a pinhead ball.

5. Let the ball travel down one of your body parts (your leg or your arm), and then imagine it traveling inside your body.

Things to Think About

- Figure out various ways to "show" where the ball is and what is the "kind" of ball—how do you communicate that information to your partner?
- Try with music. Try with a larger group.

EXERCISE 5: CIRCLES, LINES, DIAMONDS, AND CLUMPS

What you need: a small group of four or five; it can be any number, but you do need at least three for a circle to read

What's your focus: making movements for a place or spatial orientation

THE STEPS

1. Begin with forming a circle. Do a movement. It could be anything! It could be moving high to low, wiggling hips and shoulders, or turning around yourself.

2. Glide or walk into a line. It can be a straight line or a curvy line. Whatever kind of line it is you must be in the same relationship to each other. As you now move, extend legs and arms akimbo in a ragged dynamic. Then, chop or walk into:

3. A diamond orientation. Follow the person in front of you. Maybe create a side-to-side movement of the torso, or lengthening arms. But be sure to move arms to the sides where all can see—do not change your movement in such a way where it is not visible to the larger group. If you are leading, be in front of the group and communicate with them clearly.

4. Now bounce or walk into a clump. Take new action, tangle with each other and freeze when everyone feels the moment.

5. Repeat these creations with the same music or another piece of music. Keep the same choreography but listen to the music before you start so the group is all hearing the music and can gather on level ground, aurally.

Things to Think About

- You will be moving in and out of these movement configurations. You can walk simply to the next spot or move in an agreed upon dynamic. For example, glide into a line from a circle, chop to a diamond, bounce into a clump. Any order can work!

- Tempo can shift here—and remember that you don't have to move quickly just because music happens to be fast. Explore changes of dynamics.

- Try working with a great piece of classical music (Vivaldi's *Four Seasons*, perhaps), and then follow that with a jazz piece (maybe "Take Five" by Dave Brubeck). Or anything else that inspires you!

- You have made a dance exploring varied spatial formations—circle, line, diamond, clump.
- These exercises can be done in any order, so long as the group or teaching artist communicates that order clearly beforehand.

Exercises for the Beginning Choreographer

EXERCISE 1: EXPLORING CHOREOGRAPHIC STRUCTURES

What you need: mental and physical space to think and move

What's your focus: making and investigating structures and plans for the organizing movements and moments as they unfold in time and space. Here are some plans that can help inspire you:

- Create an ABA structure
- Create a canon
- Make a dance reacting to the environment
- Make a dance that's based on a call and response
- Create a rondo form
- Build a dance that uses a thought or poem in a book
- Make a dance that is related to a theme of the day
- Choreograph a dance using three clear dynamics with different body parts
- Build a dance that is directed by the musical changes or goes against the music
- Courtesy of one of our teachers: make a dance out of doodles—put on a piece of music and let yourself draw what you hear—then dance the shapes and pathways

I learned some of these exercises at courses in the Dance Education Lab at the 92Y, from Jody Arnhold and Ann Biddle. They had found a simple yet precise way of applying Rudolf Laban's movement analysis into choreography exercises for dancers and non-dancers.

Oh, and I almost forgot: it never hurts to make a dance with a clear beginning, middle, and end. Or aggressively *not*.

EXERCISE 2: NAME DANCE

What you need: a sturdy chair, music with speaker for inspiration
What's your focus: imagination and memory

THE STEPS

1. Create a dance phrase from the literal letters of your name—first name only.

2. Make shapes that relate to straight lines or curves. The order of the spelling helps to assist memory both movement and aligning with thought. You can further emphasize or create the shapes—say your name itself represents some idea like April or May. Many other cultures often have names that conceptually have meaning.

3. Try writing the letters with both arms, try with the eyes closed so that you can move from an internal place. Try to hold the last letter, shape and repeat. In repetition, the actions become a dance.

EXERCISE 3: SITE-SPECIFIC DANCE

What you need: indoor or outdoor space (during the time of COVID, creating site-related dances at home was a necessity; but no matter the outer circumstances, you can devise movement wherever you find yourself)
What's your focus: how the space itself provides opportunities for movement

THE STEPS

1. Begin with an indoor space like your home. Look around: Where do you see opportunities from movement? A wall, a table, a chair that supports your weight? A bookshelf you can make a pleasing shape next to? A corner you can disappear into, a table you can crawl under? What opportunities are there where we can improvise and set dances?

2. Choose three places. Begin to create movement that relates to each area. Make pathways between each area. Try to repeat the same way. For example, maybe I might start at the table and lean on the table in three ways. Then move in a straight line to the bookshelf. Perform two ways of leaning on the bookshelf. Then curve over to the corner, move in and away from the corner once in a clear expansion and contraction. Then move in

a circle in the center of your space, and finish with an action that reaches high.

3. Repeat your own dance for memory and choreography.

Things to Think About

Perform with different choices of music and change the ways you move as influenced by the sounds but keep the same choreography. As Stuart Hodes, a legendary dancer, partner of Martha Graham, and one of our guest artists with Dances for a Variable Population once said to one of our Movement Speaks groups, "You use the music, don't let the music use you!"

Exercises for Contact Improv

EXERCISE 1: IMPROVISING WITH YOUR WALL

What you need: a wall

What's your focus: how many ways the wall can support and liberate you

The Steps

1. Lean against the wall surface. When you feel stable, begin to lift your arms or legs, while still putting your weight against the wall's surface. Feel the support of the wall.

Contact Dance Using Wall. Photo © Meg Goldman Photography.
In photo (*L to R*) Leslie Prosterman and Erika Roth.

2. Now, still leaning, stand tilting sideways receiving support from the weight of your upper back or legs or arms. Share the energy of the wall with your body, share the exchange or stillness, allow for new balance and stretch.

3. Lean onto the wall and liberate yourself from taking all the weight. Imagine the way you look from the outside, tilting sideways and off-center.

4. Create a pathway moving across the wall with or without music, creating new, only-before-imagined shapes!

5. Add another person to the wall. Try to have a conversation in movement by relating without words with someone next to you. Copy shapes and actions. If one person is balancing with the head, try connecting with your shoulder. See how far you can tilt!

EXERCISE 2: SLOW SOFT TOUCH

What you need: a partner and space to move with them

What's your focus: attuning yourself and your movement to that of your partner

THE STEPS

1. Lightly and gently touch one hand of your partner and move in a slow way toward any direction.

2. Ask your partner to follow the movement. Continue to stay in contact, never losing touch. Experiment with the sense of back and forth. Be surprised by what happens, and surprise yourself!

3. Stretch as far as you can from the other person and dance as close as you can move, all the while find new ways to stretch and move in a close space and far space.

4. Explore the area around both your bodies. Still in contact with the fingers, allow the shifting of hands to change, use the other hand.

5. Proceed to holding both hands and practice shifts of balance with one partner lifting a leg off the floor and fluidly changing weight and balance.

Things to Think About

The dance examines the sensitivities of balance by asking for minor allowances of weight shifts, and then propelling the dance forward. Allow the body to arch, bend, stretch, and then balance each moment. Do not be afraid of the less smooth moments but aim for fluidity—aim for moments of slow soft touch.

EXERCISE 3: SHARING WEIGHT

What you need: a partner and space to move

What's your focus: the strength that comes from the counterbalance of forces between partners as they share weight

THE STEPS

1. Hold at wrists and curve pelvis away from partner. Equalize weight so both partners feel clear balance. Gently increase pull to increase stretch. Rotate hips and feel back opening, shoulder opening. Move to touching shoulders and gently "back" bend, lift sternum high and broaden collar bones. Repeat "round" back stretch and then again the "back" bend stretch. Use weight and counterpulls here.

2. Facing partner, right hand to right hand one person facing one way and the other opposite direction. Reach overhead toward partner's hand and stretch on a curve opening the left side body. Change facing and repeat. Hold left hands and reach overhead on a curve to stretch right side body.

Things to Think About

For all these stretches, the more you "give" weight and your partner counterbalances, the deeper the stretch. Try various positions of counterbalances, from moving off your own center, on a tilt, sharing weight, to supporting on an angle with variations of lifted arms and legs. Practice back and forth, one person supporting and one trying different balances, both people aware of counterbalance. Pay attention to the challenges of mobility and need for support. Hold those areas, at balance places, such as the shoulders or hips, and create movement from there. Make a dance of these efforts.

Exercises for Movement Speaks Dancers and Teachers

EXERCISE 1: SHINING SOLOS

What you need: a circle of people to witness and participate, room to dance, and some great Motown or pop music, even classical opera, as long as it makes you want to move

What's your focus: the joy of sharing your part of the dance: the dance acknowledges everyone contribution, and the people on the outside perform roles as witnesses; this designated place to perform and be you is central to Movement Speaks

THE STEPS

1. Each person, one by one, dances by themselves in the center of the circle, in the spotlight, supported by everyone surrounding that person.

2. People on the outside can dance along inspired by the person in the center of the circle, copying her moves or trying counter with their own variation. The point is to be connected to the center person's movements, to be inspired by the other.

Things to Think About

Try varying the diameter of the circle, moving closer in and pulling out. The center person feeling the support of the group, it feels different when folks are closer, more supported yet confined, farther out, more free movement. What is important is establishing the circle.

EXERCISE 2: READING BODIES

What you need: a group of four or more sitting or standing in a circle, with music or in silence

What's your focus: how movement speaks

THE STEPS

1. Gather a group together and isolate individual expressions of welcoming. We all welcome each other differently: some open their arms, some extend one hand, some simply smile directly looking at you, some

are more "flowery" in gesture, some are less ornate in movement, some bow with a twirl, some folks clearly say "hello" leaning in closer.

2. Go around the circle and say hello in movement. Experience the variety of hellos, the feelings of welcoming, the open gestures of the body.

3. Then go around the circle and say "no" with your body. A "no" gesture feels very different as coming from the person giving the gesture and getting the "no." Some people clearly cross their arms, closing off contact, some turn their backs, some back away.

Things to Think About

How much we can actually say without saying a word. I learned this exercise from dancer/choreographer Ellen Groff (a former Martha Graham dancer).

Essential Dances, Exercises, and Instructions for Being Present in Your Body

STUART DANCE

Created by the late, great, and much beloved Stuart Hodes. We miss you, Stuart!

What you need: a clear space, music with a regular and changing beat, comfortable clothes and shoes or barefoot to move

What's your focus: the challenge of balance while moving to different rhythms

THE STEPS

1. Stand still on your feet. Acknowledge the space of the room you stand in. Know your dance will take up as much space as is available to you.

2. Move side to side, shifting weight from leg to leg, then move to picking up alternate legs so you stand on one foot at a time.

3. Use the music to guide you. Use the music and the rhythm to emphasize the beats.

4. When the downbeat arrives, do a strong movement to emphasize it—lift your leg, your arms, your head. Look right and left, roll down, and touch the floor.

5. Progress to rocking front to back, all the while, illuminate the beat.

Things to Think About

- Stuart danced to the same Glenn Miller Band melody every day so he could anticipate the changes of rhythm.
- Ask yourself what kinds of movement fits, kicking your legs straight front or akimbo; or the favorite is the "Graham" move of slapping the thigh with the same arm to the side. Or you can do "the ugly," as Stuart liked to do, moving with ugly gestures and faces, in strange shapes.
- Have an ending, maybe set to a drum roll so you finish with a flourish and a still place.
- And you must, must, must take a bow.

ACKNOWLEDGMENTS

Thank you to all my teachers and fellow dancers who have taught me lessons on how to move fully, expressively, and wholeheartedly on the dance floor and in life. Thank you to our Dances for a Variable Population (DVP) Board of Directors who have helped guide our company and to the DVP staff whose heart, hard work, and dedication have meant so much to our audiences and students. And to all the innumerable DVP teachers who have expanded our Movement Speaks® program beyond what I could ever have imagined, bringing this training to so many. Some of the resources used by Movement Speaks® and in this book are developed from exercises from Dance Education Laboratory at the 92nd Street Y and Jody Gottfried Arnhold, who has been a mentor to me. Thank you to Stephanye Hunter for your guidance and belief in my story and Mindy Aloff, who first thought I might have a book in me. And to my son Noah, who has always been my biggest fan and cheered me on as I wrestled with writing sentences. And last of all to my students, who have taught me and who continue to teach and inspire me about the possibilities inherent in dance and in life. They are the beating heart of this book.

NOTES

Sensing the Mind-Body Connection

1 Thibaut, "The Mind-Body Cartesian Dualism and Psychiatry," 3.
2 Scott, "The Mind-Body Feedback Loop."
3 For additional exercises to build the mind-body connection, please see page 151.
4 Voltaire, *Questions Sur l'Encyclopédie*, 250.
5 Jhung, "About Finis Jung."
6 Jhung, "Burning Your Bridges as You Move to the Future."
7 Garrett, "Nothing Can Stop Finis Jhung from Teaching."

Discovering Balance

1 Black Mountain College, "Black Mountain College."
2 Contact Quarterly, "Contact Improvisation."
3 For exercises to explore balance, see page 153.

Stretching Myself

1 Guarino and Oliver, *Jazz Dance*.
2 For exercises to release the muscles and build mobility, see page 157.

Growing in Strength

1 Streb, *Streb*, 41
2 For exercises to build upper body strength, see page 160.
3 For exercises on picking up your feet as you walk, see page 162.

The Space We're In

1 This is a famous quote that has been passed verbally from dancer to dancer. I have yet to find it in written form. I first heard the quote from Sandra Genter, who was one of my teachers during my Barnard days. She heard it from a dancer in Cunningham's company.

2 For a series of lunge exercises based around proprioception, see page 163.

3 Slind-Flor, "Swan Lake."

Metamorphosis

1 Helena speaking of Demetrius in Act 4, Scene 1.

2 To do the exercises we developed in Venice Beach, see page 170.

3 King, *Brunelleschi's Dome.*

4 Baird and Candelario, *The Routledge Companion to Butoh Performance.*

5 Waychoff, "Butoh, Bodies, and Being."

6 For a detailed look into the Pavane for new and experienced dancers, see page 168.

Setting the Foundation

1 See page 169 for the steps to create a *Grande Finale* dance.

2 "Overview of Systemic Lupus Erythematosus (Lupus)."

Growing Upward

1 Statistics from NYC DOHMH Community Health Survey and Brookdale Health Indicators Project referenced in New York Academy of Medicine, *NYC Senior Centers,* and Campaign to End Loneliness, "Facts and Statistics."

Finding Our First Steps

1 For a deeper look at the Movement Conversation exercise, as well as a variation involving a larger group of people, see page 172.

2 For an expanded version at Beginning Improv that takes the full body into the equation, see page 174.

3 For a more detailed look at Mirroring, see page 176.

4 You can find a series of examples of Choreographic Structures on page 179.

5 To get more information about movement work with Circles, Lines, Diamonds, and Clumps, and how to lead this exercise with groups, see page 178.

Dance-Making

1 To create your own Name Dance, see page 180.

2 For instructions on how to create your own Site Specific Dance, see page 180.

3 "About Talking Band."

Contact Improvisation

1 To begin experimenting with contact improv, see page 181. There you will find exercises that use a wall, and our Slow Soft Touch exercise!

The Art of Change

1 "Overview of Peripheral Neuropathy."
2 Learn the moves to Stuart's Dance on page 185.

Exercises and Prompts for Making Dances

1 In www.dvpnyc.org and Dances for a Variable Population's YouTube channel you can find videos of exercises and dances for further reference.

BIBLIOGRAPHY

"About Talking Band." Talking Band. https://talkingband.org/new-home/ (accessed March 3, 2024).

Baird, Bruce, and Rosemary Candelario, eds. *The Routledge Companion to Butoh Performance*. London: Routledge, 2019.

Black Mountain College. "Black Mountain College: A Brief Introduction." Black Mountain College Museum + Arts Center. June 15, 2023. https://www.blackmountaincollege.org/history/.

"Facts and Statistics." Campaign to End Loneliness. https://www.campaigntoendloneliness.org/facts-and-statistics/ (accessed July 3, 2024).

Contact Quarterly. "Contact Improvisation—About." https://contactquarterly.com/contact-improvisation/about/ (accessed June 3, 2024).

Coseru, Christian. "Consciousness and the Mind-Body Problem in Indian Philosophy." In *The Routledge Handbook of Consciousness*, edited by Rocco J. Gennaro, 92–104. New York: Routledge, 2018.

Cunningham, Merce. *Changes: Notes on Choreography*. New York: The Song Cave/Merce Cunningham Trust, 2019.

Garrett, Giannella M. "Nothing Can Stop Finis Jhung from Teaching—Not Even His Recent Hip Replacement Surgery." Dance Teacher. September 29, 2017. https://dance-teacher.com/finis-jhungs-new-hip/.

Guarino, Lindsay, and Wendy Oliver, eds. *Jazz Dance: A History of the Roots and Branches*. Gainesville: University Press of Florida, 2015.

Jhung, Finis. "About Finis Jhung." https://finisjhung.com/about-finis-jhung/ (accessed January 5, 2024).

Jhung, Finis. "Burning Your Bridges as You Move to the Future." Last modified December 31, 2016. https://finisjhung.com/burning-your-bridges-as-you-move-to-the-future/.

Keogh, Martin. *Dancing Deeper Still: The Practice of Contact Improvisation*. Intimately Rooted Books, 2018.

King, Ross. *Brunelleschi's Dome: How a Renaissance Genius Reinvented Architecture*. New York: Random House, 2000.

Lesshaeve, Jacqueline. *The Dancer and the Dance; Merce Cunningham in Conversation*. London: Marion Boyars, 1991.

New York Academy of Medicine. *NYC Senior Centers: Visioning the Future*. New York: NYAM, 2010.

"Overview of Peripheral Neuropathy." Mayo Clinic. https://www.mayoclinic.org/diseases-conditions/peripheral-neuropathy/symptoms-causes/syc-20352061 (accessed March 4, 2024).

"Overview of Systemic Lupus Erythematosus (Lupus)." National Institute of Arthritis and Musculoskeletal and Skin Diseases. https://www.niams.nih.gov/health-topics/lupus (accessed March 1, 2024).

Scott, Maiken. "The Mind-Body Feedback Loop." Interview with Ignite Sadhana, William Breitbart, Stephanie Foo, and Liz Tung. *The Pulse,* NPR, May 19, 2023. Podcast. https://www.npr.org/2023/05/18/1176839299/the-mind-body-feedback-loop.

Slind-Flor, Victoria. "Swan Lake." *Journal American* (Bellevue, WA), April 10, 1981, C1–2.

Srinivasan, T. M. "From Meditation to Dhyana." *International Journal of Yoga* 6, no. 1 (2013): 1–3.

Streb, Elizabeth. *Streb: How to Become an Extreme Action Hero.* New York: Feminist Press at CUNY, 2020.

Thibaut, Florence. 2018a. "The Mind-Body Cartesian Dualism and Psychiatry." *Dialogues in Clinical Neuroscience* 20 (1): 3.

Voltaire. *Questions Sur l'Encyclopédie, Par Des Amateurs.* Geneva: 1770.

Waychoff, Brianne. "Butoh, Bodies, and Being." *Kaleidoscope: A Graduate Journal of Qualitative Communication Research* 8.4 (2009): 37–53.

INDEX

INDEX OF EXERCISES AND PROMPTS FOR MAKING DANCES

Stretching

Naomi Goldberg Haas is the founder and artistic director of Dances for a Variable Population. A leader in the field of creative aging, she also founded the intergenerational dance company Los Angeles Modern Dance & Ballet. She danced with Pacific Northwest Ballet and holds a BA from Barnard College and an MFA from Tisch Dance/NYU. Goldberg Haas received the New York State Dance Education Association Lifetime Impact in Dance Education award in recognition of her extraordinary impact on the dance education community.

Mikhaela Mahony is a Brooklyn-based director working at the intersection of theater, opera, and film. Mikhaela received her BA in English and creative writing from Barnard College, and her MFA in theater directing from Columbia University under the tutelage of Brian Kulick and Anne Bogart. She is a proud member of New York City's Ensemble Studio Theatre.